★ The Korean War ★

STRATEGIC BATTLES

Titles in the American War Library series include:

The Korean War
Life as a POW
Life of an American Soldier
The War at Home
Weapons of War

The American Revolution
The Civil War
The Cold War
The Persian Gulf War
The Vietnam War
The War on Terrorism
World War II

AMERICAN
WAR LIBRARY

★ ★ ★ ★

★ The Korean War ★

STRATEGIC BATTLES

by Craig E. Blohm

LUCENT
BOOKS®

THOMSON
————★————™
GALE

San Diego • Detroit • New York • San Francisco • Cleveland • New Haven, Conn. • Waterville, Maine • London • Munich

© 2004 by Lucent Books. Lucent Books is an imprint of The Gale Group, Inc.,
a division of Thomson Learning, Inc.

Lucent Books® and Thomson Learning™ are trademarks used herein under license.

For more information, contact
Lucent Books
27500 Drake Rd.
Farmington Hills, MI 48331-3535
Or you can visit our Internet site at http://www.gale.com

LIBRARY OF CONGRESS CATALOGING-IN-PUBLICATION DATA

Blohm, Craig E., 1948–
   Strategic battles / by Craig E. Blohm.
     p. cm. — (American war library. Korean War)
Summary: Discusses some of the strategic battles of the Korean Conflict, including the
Battle of Osan, the amphibious assault at Inchon, and the Battle of Pork Chop Hill.
Includes bibliographical references and index.
    ISBN 1-59018-261-8 (hardback: alk. paper)
1. Korean War, 1950–1953—Participation, American—Juvenile literature. 2. United
States—Armed Forces—Korea—Juvenile literature. 3. United States. Army—History—
Korean War, 1950–1953—Juvenile literature. [1. Korean War, 1950–1953—Campaigns.]
I. Title. II. Series.
   DS919.B56 2004
   951.904'1242—dc22
                                                  2003013869

★ Contents ★

A Nation Forged by War

The United States, like many nations, was forged and defined by war. Despite Benjamin Franklin's opinion that "There never was a good war or a bad peace," the United States owes its very existence to the War of Independence, one to which Franklin wholeheartedly subscribed. The country forged by war in 1776 was tempered and made stronger by the Civil War in the 1860s.

The Texas Revolution, the Mexican-American War, and the Spanish-American War expanded the country's borders and gave it overseas possessions. These wars made the United States a world power, but this status came with a price, as the nation became a key but reluctant player in both World War I and World War II.

Each successive war further defined the country's role on the world stage. Following World War II, U.S. foreign policy redefined itself to focus on the role of defender, not only of the freedom of its own citizens, but also of the freedom of people everywhere. During the Cold War that followed World War II until the collapse of the Soviet Union, defending the world meant fighting communism. This goal, manifested in the Korean and Vietnam conflicts, proved elusive and soured the American public on its achievability. As the United States emerges as the world's sole superpower, American foreign policy has been guided less by national interest and more by protecting international human rights. But as involvement in Somalia and Kosovo proves, this goal has been equally elusive.

As a result, the country's view of itself changed. Bolstered by victories in World Wars I and II, Americans first relished the role of protector. But, as war followed war in a seemingly endless procession, Americans began to doubt their leaders, their motives, and themselves. The Vietnam War especially caused people to question the validity of sending its young people to die in places where they were not particularly wanted and for people who did not seem especially grateful.

While the most obvious changes brought about by America's wars have been geopolitical in nature, many other aspects of society have been touched. War often does not bring about change directly, but acts instead like the catalyst in a chemical reaction, accelerating changes already in progress.

Some of these changes have been societal. The role of women in the United States had been slowly changing, but World War II put thousands into the work force and into uniform. They might have gone back to being housewives after the war, but equality, once experienced, would not be forgotten.

Likewise, wars have accelerated technological change. The necessity for faster airplanes and more destructive bombs led to the development of jet planes and nuclear energy. Artificial fibers developed for parachutes in the 1940s were used in clothing of the 1950s.

Lucent Books' American War Library covers key wars in the development of the nation. Each war is covered in several volumes, to allow for more detail, context, and to provide volumes on often neglected subjects, such as the kamikazes of World War II, or the weapons used in the Civil War. As with all Lucent books, notes, annotated bibliographies, and appendixes such as glossaries give students a launching point for further research. In addition, sidebars and archival photographs enhance the text. Together, each volume in the American War Library will aid students in understanding how America's wars have shaped and changed its politics, economics, and society.

The Forgotten War

The Korean War occupies a unique place in U.S. military history. It was not as devastating as the Civil War, nor did it inspire unabashed patriotism as did World War II. It was not as divisive as Vietnam, nor as swift as Operation Iraqi Freedom. It has been called by some the forgotten war, and by others the first war, America lost. Officially it was not even a war, but, as President Harry S. Truman called it, a "police action" in which the United States and its United Nations (UN) allies were helping to police democratic South Korea against incursions from Communist North Korea. But for the men who fought battles with such names as Osan, the Pusan Perimeter, the Chosin Reservoir, and Pork Chop Hill, the Korean War will always remain a time of testing, of courage under fire, when your buddy got killed but you had to carry on.

In all wars, it is the action on the battlefield that ultimately determines the success or failure of each military campaign. Generals can carefully plan their strategy from the relative safety of their headquarters behind the lines, but it is up to the officers and men in the field to turn that strategy into triumph or defeat. The battles of the Korean War led not to a stunning victory, but to an uneasy deadlock that left the two sides where they had been at the beginning of the war. Unlike the Pacific theater in World War II, where the Allied forces went island-hopping right up to Japan's doorstep, in Korea gains made by one side were inevitably turned back by the other.

Each of the battles presented in this book had a unique significance in the Korean War. The destruction of Task Force Smith at the Battle of Osan showed the United States that the war in Korea would not be the cakewalk that was expected at the outset. At Inchon, a daring amphibious landing displayed the brilliance of General Douglas MacArthur and turned the tide of war for the first time. As the North Koreans pushed the UN forces into a last stronghold called the Pusan Perimeter, only a courageous effort to hold and then break out of the perimeter prevented an early end to the war and a victory for the Communists. The combination of the Inchon landing and the Pusan Perimeter breakout had the North Koreans on the run, and victory for the UN looked sure. Then came the surprise entry into the war of thousands of Chinese soldiers. The battle of the Chinese against the UN at Unsan was the first military clash between communism and democracy to take place during the ideological battle known as the Cold War.

Some politicians predicted it would be the beginning of World War III. But once the Chinese threat was taken seriously by military leaders, the UN learned that it could hold its own against the Communists, as the battle for the strategically located town of Chipyong proved. One of the most famous encounters of the Korean War, the Battle of the Chosin Reservoir, pitted the U.S. Marines against overwhelming numbers of Chinese troops. That the marines were able to escape after being surrounded and then to evacuate them-

A U.S. Marine charges forward as an artillery shell explodes. The UN's ground attack proved crucial during the latter half of the Korean War.

selves and nearly a hundred thousand Korean refugees is a testament to the courage of the Marine Corps.

All these battles took place in the first year of the war, when both Communist and UN forces experienced a series of swift victories followed by crushing defeats. The last two years of the Korean War were marked by discord at the on-again, off-again peace talks and a stalemate on the battlefield. The Battle of Pork Chop Hill typified the bloody yet futile combat of the final years of the war, when unimportant, strategically useless hills became bargaining chips in the peace negotiations. Peace eventually came, but at a high price.

Was Korea really the first war that the United States lost? At the beginning of the war, the 38th parallel separated North and South Korea; at the end, that line still stood —and does so to this day. That the Communists, however, were thwarted in their attempt to unite the country under their political system may be counted as a victory for the United States and its UN allies. Will Korea remain the forgotten war? For the sake of the 33,741 Americans who gave their lives in the fight for freedom, one must hope that is not the case.

Conflict in Korea

Saturday, June 24, 1950, was hot and humid in Independence, Missouri, a typical early summer day in the hometown of President Harry S. Truman. The president had arrived in Independence that afternoon to enjoy a weekend visit with his family, an all-too-brief respite from the cares and pressures of Washington, D.C. Truman was happy to be home and cheerfully greeted a small crowd that had gathered outside his house. Later, after dinner, the family retired to the screened porch for a bit of pleasant conversation. It was just the kind of relaxing interlude that Truman, who was beginning his fifth year as president, needed.

Just before 9:30 the telephone rang. It was Secretary of State Dean Acheson, and the news he was bringing would abruptly end Truman's idyllic weekend. "Mr. President," Acheson said, "I have very serious news. The North Koreans have invaded South Korea." Truman was shaken by the call and, according to his daughter Mar-

garet, "made it clear, from the moment he heard the news, that he feared this was the opening of World War III." The next afternoon Truman boarded his airplane *Independence* and took off for Washington, arriving at about 7:15 P.M. For photographers who gathered at the airport to photograph the presidential arrival, Truman had few words. "That's all," he said. "We've got a job to do."[1]

Prelude to Conflict

The Korean War had its origins in the last global conflict, World War II, and with Truman's predecessor in the White House, Franklin D. Roosevelt. As that war was slowly winding down in early 1945, Roosevelt met with British and Soviet leaders to plan for a postwar world. One of the decisions to be made was what to do about Korea, an ancient Asian nation that had been under Japanese occupation since 1910. With Japan heading for defeat at the hands of the Allied forces, it was decided that the United States and the Soviet Union together would guide Korea toward its new postwar status as an independent nation. But when Soviet troops descended on Korea from the north, the United States became concerned that they would ultimately overrun the entire Korean peninsula. To prevent this, the United States drew an imaginary line dividing Korea at the 38th parallel, at about the middle of the peninsula. Above this line the Communist nation of North Korea was established, supported by the Soviet Union. Below the parallel was the democratic nation of South Korea, backed by the United States. The line was intended to be only a temporary measure until elections could be arranged to unite the country. But it did not turn out that way.

Heading North Korea's Communist government was Premier Kim Il Sung, while Syngman Rhee was elected president of South Korea. For a while U.S. and Soviet troops remained in these new nations,

---

U.S. Marines board the ship that will transport them to South Korea. President Harry S. Truman sent troops to South Korea after the Communist North Korean People's Army crossed the 38th parallel in June 1950.

building up armies so that they could provide for their own national security. But gradually the troops were withdrawn and by 1950 only a few military advisers were left. Both Kim Il Sung and Syngman Rhee wanted to see Korea united once again, Kim under communism and Rhee under democracy. Kim Il Sung, with the backing of the Soviet Union, would make the first move to try to turn that desire into a reality.

A United Nations War

The situation that caused Secretary Acheson to phone the president on that warm Saturday evening was as serious as the president had imagined. On June 25, 1950 (Korean time), the North Korean People's Army (NKPA) had crossed the 38th parallel and invaded South Korea. In the next few days, as the North Korean troops and tanks rolled over the countryside, it became clear that the South Korean army was no match for the well-equipped and well-trained NKPA. To prevent a swift takeover of South Korea, Truman authorized sending U.S. troops to the Korean peninsula. "I don't want to go to war,"[2] the president said, but in the end he knew he had to make that choice. Truman understood that to deny help to a friendly democratic nation would send the wrong message to other U.S. allies. So the United States was once more at war. But it was not alone.

The end of World War II had seen the creation of the United Nations (UN), an international body dedicated to fostering cooperation among nations, interna-

tional peace, and human rights. Soon after the invasion, an emergency session of the UN Security Council prepared a resolution calling for North Korea to end its aggression against South Korea. The Soviet Union, a member of the Security Council, would surely have vetoed the resolution if it had not been boycotting the council meetings over UN refusal to seat China, another Communist nation. So the resolution passed and, for the first time, the UN went to war to stop aggression against one of its members. General Douglas MacArthur, a veteran military leader and commander of the American forces in Japan, was made supreme commander of all the UN forces in Korea.

The Conflict Begins

With the element of surprise on its side, as well as weapons and equipment supplied by the Soviet Union, the NKPA had little trouble overwhelming the military force of South Korea (officially known as the Republic of Korea, or ROK). When the United States entered the conflict, its troops fared little better. The soldiers closest to Korea were occupation troops stationed in Japan. Softened by an easy life in Japan and hampered by a lack of combat experience, the first U.S. soldiers to enter the Korean War were no better matched against the North Koreans than were the ROK troops. Early battles brought disaster to the American units sent to rescue South Korean troops who were fleeing from the NKPA.

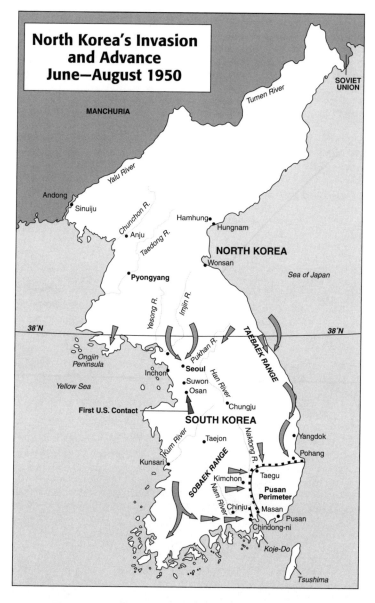

North Korea's Invasion and Advance June–August 1950

MANCHURIA

SOVIET UNION

Tumen River

Yalu River

Andong

Sinuiju

Chunchon R.

Anju

Hamhung

Hungnam

Taedong R.

NORTH KOREA

Wonsan

Pyongyang

Sea of Japan

Yesong R.

Imjin R.

38°N

38°N

Ongjin Peninsula

Pukhan R.

Seoul

Inchon

Suwon

Osan

Han River

TAEBAEK RANGE

Yellow Sea

Chungju

First U.S. Contact

SOUTH KOREA

Kum River

Taejon

Naktong R.

Yangdok

Kunsari

SOBAEK RANGE

Pohang

Kimchon

Taegu

Nam River

Pusan Perimeter

Chinju

Masan

Pusan

Chindong-ni

Koje-Do

Tsushima

tirely. If that had happened, the war would have been over almost before it began. By early August, however, UN forces gained some strength and managed to halt the North Korean advance. They were trapped, however, in the Pusan Perimeter, a five-thousand-square-mile area surrounding the port city of Pusan at the far southeastern tip of Korea. The NKPA had the Pusan Perimeter under constant attack and was threatening to break through and finish its job of conquest.

Because the perimeter surrounded Pusan, South Korea's main seaport, reinforcements of men and equipment were arriving daily. As soon as the UN forces were strengthened enough, they could try to break out of the perimeter and push the North Koreans back. To aid in this effort to beat back the North Koreans, MacArthur hatched a daring plan. He would launch an amphibious landing behind enemy lines at a port named Inchon while the troops at the Pusan Perimeter would stage their breakout. The North Korean army would be trapped between these two forces and annihilated.

Despite additional UN troops pouring into Korea, it seemed that nothing could stop the North Korean advance. UN forces, steadily driven back, were in danger of being pushed off the peninsula en-

The plan was a success, and the NKPA was pushed past the 38th parallel back into North Korea. This stunning reversal of the war led to a dilemma: With the North Korean army retreating, should the UN keep advancing north and create a united, democratic Korea? The answer was yes, and with it, the stage was set for another reversal of fortune—this time for the United Nations Command.

An Unexpected Foe

If the United Nations Command had only the North Korean People's Army to fight, the Korean War might have ended in late 1950. Total victory seemed at hand as NKPA troops retreated toward the Yalu River, the boundary between North Korea and its northern neighbor, the Chinese province of Manchuria. But lurking just beyond the Yalu were thousands of Chinese soldiers, and they were preparing to join the war on the North Korean side.

Chinese Foreign Minister Chou En-lai had warned that his nation would intervene if UN troops crossed the 38th parallel. Chou's warning was dismissed by U.S. officials, including General MacArthur, as merely a bluff. But it was not a bluff, and in October 1950 nearly two hundred thousand Chinese troops quietly crossed the Yalu River under cover of darkness, taking

A U.S. Army tank crew scouts for enemy targets in the Pusan Perimeter. In the opening phase of the war, UN forces concentrated on defending the perimeter from the North Korean advance.

up positions in the rugged hills of North Korea. Although China called these troops "volunteers," they were in fact highly trained soldiers of the Chinese People's Liberation Army—China's regular army. The American military referred to them as the Chinese Communist Forces, or CCF.

The clashes between UN forces and the CCF were a disaster for the UN. Near the town of Unsan, U.S. and ROK units were destroyed, sending the survivors retreating. The UN's northward advance was halted when Chinese overwhelmed the UN Command with sheer numbers and their use of night attacks, roadblocks, and flanking maneuvers to surround the enemy. By January 1951 the UN forces had been pushed back south of the 38th parallel and the war, which MacArthur had promised would end in victory by Christmas, was now destined to drag on at a cost of mounting casualties and continued devastation of the Korean landscape.

Stalemate

Soon the United Nations Command began a new drive north toward the 38th parallel. Seoul, the South Korean capital, became a symbol of the seesaw nature of the Korean War. Captured in the initial attack by the North Koreans in June 1950, it was retaken by UN forces after the Inchon landing, only to be lost once more when the Chinese entered the war. In March 1951 UN troops recaptured Seoul, the last time the city would change hands. With renewed confidence, UN forces

pushed the Chinese back across the 38th parallel and once again faced the question of advancing toward the Yalu. But if the UN decided to push on, China would simply send in more troops to counter the UN advance. In turn, the UN would have to supply more soldiers of its own to meet the challenge. "We could have pushed right on to the Yalu in the spring of 1951," recalled General Matthew Ridgway, commander of the Eighth Army at that time. "The price for such a drive would have been far too high for what we would have gained, however. We would have lost heavily in dead and wounded—my estimate at the time was 100,000. [Would the American people] commit themselves to an endless war in the bottomless pit of the Asian mainland? I thought then and I think now that the answer to these questions was 'No.'"[3]

It was obvious that the Korean War could drag on indefinitely with neither side able to claim victory. The time had come to pursue peace.

Peace Talks and POWs

By the spring of 1951 the Korean War was at a standstill reminiscent of the trench warfare of World War I. The two sides faced off from trenches dug into the Korean countryside, creating a front called the Main Line of Resistance (MLR) that stretched from east to west across the middle of the peninsula. There was little movement of the front as firefights were conducted between outposts located along the MLR. For the next two years the front line of the Korean War would remain unchanged.

While the outpost fighting continued, peace talks were getting under way. On July 10, 1951, delegates from both sides met in the North Korean city of Kaesong to begin negotiations to end the war. From the outset the delegates argued about everything, from trivialities such as the delegates' chairs to important matters such as troop withdrawal and the location of a "demilitarized zone" between the two nations. Head UN delegate Admiral C. Turner Joy scolded the North Koreans for being overly contentious: "By your . . . refusal to negotiate you have brought these meetings to a standstill. You have slammed every door leading to possible progress."[4] On August 23 the Communists broke off the peace talks.

Throughout the summer and early fall, bloodshed continued on the battlefield. Two areas, Heartbreak Ridge and Bloody Ridge, saw especially tough combat. When peace negotiations finally resumed in October 1951, the location had been changed to Panmunjom, a town a few miles east of Kaesong. By December the talks turned to the subject of prisoners of war (POWs). Lists of POWs were drawn up, showing the UN holding 133,000 prisoners and the Communists accounting for 11,500, a figure that the UN disputed as too low. Eventually an agreement was reached on the exchange of prisoners, but soon a stumbling block threatened to stall the talks once more.

Many of the prisoners held by the UN did not want to be repatriated, that is, returned to live under the repressive and often cruel regimes of their Communist homelands of China and North Korea. The United States insisted that it would not send any POW back to a Communist country if he did not want to go. The Communists were just as adamant that all prisoners had to be returned to their homelands. Once more the negotiations were at a stalemate and the talks were suspended; they would not resume until the spring of 1953.

Last-Minute Obstacles

With the death of Soviet dictator Joseph Stalin in March 1953, the Communists became more willing to do what was necessary to end the Korean War. In April they agreed to Operation Little Switch, a plan to send home all sick and wounded POWs. The exchange went smoothly, with some 6,600 prisoners released by the UN and 684 by the Communists. The fate of the other POWs was still under discussion at the peace talks.

Soon another crisis threatened to destroy the talks—a crisis created by South Korean president Syngman Rhee. Rhee had never been in favor of a divided Korea; he kept alive his dream of uniting Korea under his own constitutional government. He had done his best to undermine the talks through radio broadcasts and public rallies. Now, as the negotiations approached a successful conclusion,

Sacking MacArthur

Although General Douglas MacArthur was the commander in chief of the UN forces in Korea, he did have a superior whom he was required to report to: the president of the United States, Harry S. Truman. Unfortunately, the two men held different opinions on the extent of MacArthur's authority to run the war in Korea. It was a situation that ultimately would leave Truman no choice but to remove MacArthur from his command.

In the spring of 1951, as the Eighth Army was advancing toward the 38th parallel, Truman felt that the time was right to begin pursuing peace in Korea. He decided to announce to the Chinese that the UN would consider a cease-fire, and the State Department drafted an official statement to that effect. On March 20 MacArthur was told about the statement and informed that there should be no further advance past the 38th parallel to allow the diplomatic offer to take its course. But before the official statement could be broadcast, MacArthur issued his own statement, threatening the Chinese with utter destruction if they did not accept UN peace terms. According to Bevin Alexander in his book *Korea: The First War We Lost*, MacArthur's action "ranks among the most blatant acts in history of a field commander defying the instructions of superior authority and the established policy of the nation he serves." Truman's official proposal had to be shelved, lest it cause confusion about the true intentions of the United States.

MacArthur's insubordination could not be ignored. According to Alexander, Truman later called it "an act totally disregarding all directives to abstain from any declaration on foreign policy. It was in open defiance of my orders as President and as commander in chief." After meeting with Secretary of State Dean Acheson and the Joint Chiefs of Staff (who had their own misgivings about MacArthur's military judgment), Truman made the decision: MacArthur would be fired. On April 10, 1951, Truman signed the orders relieving MacArthur of his command; they were delivered to the general the next day. General Matthew B. Ridgway, commander of the Eighth Army, took over MacArthur's duties as commander of the UN forces.

Douglas MacArthur returned home to a hero's welcome. Later, at a joint meeting of Congress, MacArthur quoted a line from an old army song, a passage that would forever be linked to the general: "Old soldiers never die, they just fade away."

General Douglas MacArthur (left) and President Truman pose together in 1950. Truman later relieved MacArthur of his command for insubordination.

Rhee threatened to remove his ROK forces from UN control and continue fighting the war on his own. "We will decide our own fate," Rhee defiantly proclaimed. "We do not ask anyone to fight for us."[5] It was an empty threat, for it should have been obvious even to Rhee that the ROK soldiers did not stand a chance against the CCF without U.S. help.

Rhee had other disruptive tactics in mind, and soon he imposed a more serious obstacle. Throughout the talks, the UN had stood firm on its decision not to repatriate North Koreans who no longer wished to live under a Communist regime.

Eventually, however, the United States agreed to a new Communist proposal that those POWs be released to a neutral nation.

Rhee was against this plan. Shortly after midnight on June 18, 1953, Rhee allowed some twenty-five thousand prisoners of war to simply walk out of South Korean POW camps and escape into the countryside, instead of being handed over to a neutral nation as had been agreed. "The gate was wide open," a U.S. sergeant at the POW camp remembered, "and the North Korean prisoners were running through on the double, carrying their ditty bags." When the sergeant asked a

Survivors' Story

The NKPA was a professional, well trained fighting force, but it was not above treating its prisoners of war with cruelty. As the men of the Eighth Army moved north in October 1950, they discovered evidence of North Korean brutality. The story is related in this excerpt from *Korea: The First War We Lost* by Bevin Alexander:

> The Eighth Army advance force moving up the road from Pyongyang to Sunchon encountered few enemy soldiers. But the assistant commander of the 1st Cavalry Division, Brigadier General Frank A. Allen, Jr., and his party discovered a sad and sickening sight: around a railroad tunnel near Myongucham, about five miles northwest of Sunchon, were the bodies of sixty-six American POWs who had been murdered and seven more American POWs who had either starved to death or died of disease. In addition, General Allen and his party found twenty-three Americans who had escaped from their North Korean captors, some of them critically wounded. . . .
>
> The survivors told the story: two trains, each carrying about 150 American POWs, left Pyongyang on October 17. . . . These were survivors of a group of 370 Americans the North Koreans had marched north from Seoul shortly after the Inchon landing. Each day five or six Americans died of dysentery, starvation or exposure. Their bodies were removed from the train. A few Americans escaped along the way. On October 20 . . . the second of the two trains remained in the Myongucham tunnel. It still had about 100 Americans, crowded into open coal gondolas and boxcars. That evening, the North Korean guards took the Americans in three groups to get their evening meal. The North Koreans shot them down as they waited for it. Most of the Americans who survived did so by feigning death. The guards and the train left that night.

A landing craft transports Communist POWs to be exchanged for UN POWs during Operation Big Switch.

ROK guard what was going on, "He just shrugged and smiled."[6]

U.S. officials quickly made it clear to the Communist negotiators that Rhee had acted alone and that the United States still sought peace at the negotiating table. Fortunately, the crisis passed with U.S. assurances that such incidents would not happen again.

The End

After much persuasion and assurances of massive military and financial aid from the United States, Syngman Rhee eventually dropped his objections to the armistice. He stated that "we shall not obstruct it, so long as no measures or actions taken under the armistice are detrimental to our national survival."[7] On July 27, 1953, the delegates at Panmunjom signed an armistice agreement ending the Korean War. On August 5, Operation Big Switch began, overseeing the exchange of all remaining prisoners of war. From its beginning to

21

the conclusion of the operation on September 6, the Communists released 12,773 UN prisoners, and the UN freed 75,823 Communist POWs. Of the latter number, 22,600 prisoners refused to return to their homelands and were handed over to the Neutral Nations Repatriation Committee, which decided where the ex-POWs would ultimately settle.

The Korean War was a costly conflict for both sides. U.S. casualties included 33,741 deaths (killed in action, died of wounds, and declared dead after being captured or missing in action). In addition, there were 2,835 nonhostile deaths and more than 103,000 wounded. Ironically, of those killed on the battlefield,

12,300 died during the last two years of the war—years when peace talks were traversing their on-again, off-again course. Communist losses are more difficult to substantiate, but estimates range up to 1.5 million killed and wounded, nearly two-thirds of whom were Chinese. Yet for all the death and destruction the Korean War brought, in the end the line between North and South Korea remained unchanged.

In the beginning, in the early summer of 1950, that line was about to be crossed. America would be called upon to restore the line, and it would send its young men thousands of miles from home to do the job.

Chapter 2

Task Force Smith: First Blood

At about four o'clock on the rainy morning of June 25, 1950, the thundering roar of artillery split the dark skies of Korea. Beginning in the west and continuing eastward, the artillery barrage soon became a continuous reverberation along the 38th parallel, the dividing line between North and South Korea. Within an hour troops of the North Korean People's Army (NKPA) began advancing under protection of the artillery fire. The invasion of South Korea, the first hostilities of the Korean War, had begun.

At Camp Wood near the city of Kumamoto in Japan, U.S. Army Private First Class Robert Roy was enjoying a restful weekend. Five years after the end of World War II, occupation duty in Japan was an easy assignment. "Everything was cheap," recalled Roy. "You could go on liberty every night. If you were off duty, you were gone. There were bars and movie theaters and cabarets where you

could drink beer and talk with the girls."[8] On Sunday morning of June 25, 1950, with no duty scheduled for the weekend, nineteen-year-old Roy slept late.

Roy's sleep would not be disturbed that morning. Indeed, over the next several days he was unaware of the events in Korea. After all, lowly privates were rarely told anything in advance. On June 30 Roy and his comrades returned to their barracks after a night out on the town. "We'd just gotten to bed," he remembered, "when one of our lieutenants came in, threw on the lights and said, 'Pack your gear. We're headed for Korea.' That's when I knew the war was on."[9]

Invasion

The North Korean troops that led the advance across the 38th parallel were part of a massive invasion force that totaled some 90,000 North Korean soldiers (out of a total army of about 135,000). Efficiently organized and rigidly disciplined,

the NKPA troops were equipped with nearly 200 aircraft and 150 Russian-made T-34 tanks. Well trained by the Soviet Union, the NKPA was a formidable fighting machine.

On the other side of the 38th parallel the army of Republic of Korea (ROK) was in no shape to halt the North Korean assault. When Syngman Rhee became president of the ROK in 1948, he made it known that he favored a united Korea and would use military force if necessary in order to achieve that goal. To discourage Rhee's ambitions, the United States kept his army weak and underequipped.

Thousands of South Korean refugees flee their homes after an estimated ninety thousand North Korean soldiers crossed the 38th parallel.

ROK soldiers were mostly illiterate and inexperienced in combat, and their officers were often incompetent and corrupt. Although American advisers of the Korean Military Advisory Group (KMAG) had been training the ROK soldiers, the language barrier made their task difficult at best.

When the NKPA pushed forward into South Korea on six invasion routes along the length of the 38th parallel, the ROK forces were taken completely by surprise. Some ROK soldiers had never even seen a tank, and in any event their weapons were useless against the T-34's heavy armor. ROK soldiers retreated in panic, abandoning equipment and weapons as North Korean soldiers and tanks overran their outposts. Seoul, the capital of South Korea, fell on June 27, triggering a mass exodus of civilians, hundreds of whom died when bridges over the Han River were prematurely destroyed by fleeing ROK troops. By the end of June, as the shattered ROK army tried to regroup, it seemed that nothing could stop the NKPA from pushing all the way to the southern end of the Korean peninsula.

General Douglas MacArthur, the commander of Allied occupation forces in Japan, evaluated the situation in Korea and sent a message to Washington: "It is essential that the enemy advance be held or its impetus will threaten the overrunning of all Korea. . . . The only assurance for holding the present line and the ability to regain later the lost ground is the introduction of United States ground combat forces into the Korean battle area."[10] MacArthur ordered General William F. Dean, commander of the Twenty-fourth Division, to quickly prepare a force to go to Korea.

Task Force Smith

In 1950 Lieutenant Colonel Charles Bradley Smith was commander of the First Battalion, Twenty-first Infantry Regiment of the Twenty-fourth Division, a part of the U.S. occupation forces in Japan. "Brad" Smith, as he was often called, was a veteran of World War II who had witnessed the Japanese attack on Pearl Harbor, Hawaii. On July 1 Brad Smith received his orders from General Dean, instructions that were concise but not very detailed. "When you get to Pusan," the general told Smith, "head for Taejon. We want to stop the North Koreans as far from Pusan as possible. Contact General Church. If you can't locate him, go to Taejon and beyond if you can. Sorry I can't give you more information. That's all I've got. Good luck to you and God bless you and your men."[11]

The job of Task Force Smith, as Smith's group would soon be named, was to reinforce the ROKs fighting against the NKPA, delaying the rapidly advancing North Koreans until more U.S. troops could arrive. Colonel Smith's hastily assembled group consisted of about 440 soldiers, of which only 406 would be in the first wave heading to Korea. The task force was made up of two rifle companies (both undermanned), half of a headquarters company and communications platoon, and a heavy weapons platoon armed with six bazookas, two recoilless rifles, and six mortars. Most of the men under Smith's command were twenty years old or younger, and few had combat experience. This small contingent of soldiers would be, in MacArthur's words, an "arrogant display of strength to fool the enemy into a belief that I had more resources at my disposal than I did."[12] To Smith, it just might have seemed a suicide mission.

Task Force Smith flew from Japan to Korea in six C-54 transport aircraft, landing at Pusan in South Korea on the afternoon of July 1, 1950. Crowds of South Koreans cheered and bands played as the men boarded trains for the twelve-hour ride to Taejon, a town 125 miles north of Pusan. With Task Force Smith was Private Bob Roy. "At Taejon we loaded onto trucks," he recalled, "and from there we moved a little farther each day. I had no idea where we were going. All I knew is that we were headed for the front."[13] Where they were headed was a town called Osan, some twenty-five miles from Seoul. About three miles north of the town Smith found a strategic ridge overlooking the main highway and a railroad leading to Seoul. Here was a likely path that the NKPA would take on its drive southward. And it was here that Task Force Smith would make its stand.

Osan

On July 4, 1950, Smith's small force was joined by Battery A of the Fifty-second Field Artillery Battalion, which contributed the firepower of six 105mm howitzers manned by 108 soldiers. Later that day Smith received word that his task force was to "take up . . . good positions near Osan."[14] Loading onto Korean trucks and other vehicles, Smith's men moved out. By 3:00 A.M. on July 5, Task Force Smith reached its destination and the men began to dig in. The infantry deployed along the ridge straddling the highway, and the recoilless rifles and mortars were set up. But their equipment was old and in poor condition. "We used World War II leftovers," said one lieutenant, "and much of our gear and equipment was shabby."[15]

Several thousand yards behind the front line of infantrymen, the gunners of the Fifty-second set up their howitzers. They had about twelve hundred rounds of high-explosive ammunition for the howitzers, but only six of these were high-explosive antitank (HEAT) rounds capable of penetrating heavy tank armor. HEAT rounds were hard to come by—there were only eighteen in all Japan—and all six were given to a howitzer stationed about halfway between the infantry and the other artillery. By dawn on July 5 it was raining and the men of Task Force Smith were dug in, nervously expecting the arrival of the NKPA. They would not have long to wait.

Private Roy, who was part of a 75mm recoilless rifle crew up at the infantry position, was about to begin eating his breakfast: "About seven in the morning I decided to open a can of C rations, and that's when we saw the tanks. I just dropped the can. . . . We didn't realize what we'd gotten into until we saw those tanks. But by then we were in it."[16] The first wave of North Korean armor that came down the road was a column of eight Russian-built

T-34 tanks. For thirty minutes Brad Smith watched the tanks as they lumbered into artillery range. At 8:16 A.M. the Fifty-second opened fire with its 105mm howitzers, initiating the first U.S. battle of the Korean War. But as the artillery shells began exploding around their targets, the tanks just kept rolling forward, heedless of the artillery fire.

The enemy tanks began firing their cannons and machine guns in the general direction of the U.S. position, not even bothering to aim at their ineffectual enemy. Lieutenant Colonel Smith, seeing that the artillery barrage was not working, told his recoilless rifle teams to hold fire until the tanks came within seven hundred yards of their positions. When the lead tank finally rolled within range, the recoilless rifles opened fire. "We fired as fast as we could," remembered Bob Roy. "As soon as we'd get a round into the breech we'd cover our ears and let it go, get another one in, fire that one . . . but they went right through us, right on down the road."[17] Bazooka fire from as close as fifteen yards also had no effect, not even direct hits at the rear of the tanks where their armor was weakest. It seemed as if nothing could stop the T-34s.

As the tanks advanced past the infantry position, the 105mm howitzer with the HEAT ammunition began to fire. The antitank shells finally were able to damage the two lead tanks, which pulled to the side of the road so as not to block the way for the rest of the armored column.

Ordinary Heroes

Most of the men who fought in Korea were not career soldiers but simply ordinary guys who were called on to fight in the defense of freedom. It is a tribute to the American spirit that such ordinary people can display uncommon courage in the face of danger. Task Force Smith at Osan was one of the many units filled with these "ordinary heroes." Joseph Goulden tells of two such men in his book, *Korea: The Untold Story of the Korean War*:

> Novice though they were, the defenders fought valiantly. Private First Class Vern Mulligan had the tripod of his machine gun shot away by enemy fire. He propped the barrel across an empty ammunition box and continued firing. More fire demolished this makeshift prop, and six North Korean soldiers ran toward him. Mulligan draped the gun across his forearm and fired. He killed all six.
>
> A first lieutenant, Raymond "Bodie" Adams, had pitched for the regimental baseball team back in Japan. Now he threw the most important pitch of his career. He tossed a grenade the seemingly impossible distance of forty yards, square into a North Korean machine-gun position, destroying the gun and killing the crew.

One of the tanks immediately caught fire. When the crew jumped out, two men raised their hands in surrender, but a third came out shooting. Before he was killed by U.S. troops, his fire struck an American machine gunner, the first U.S. soldier to die in the war.

The six HEAT rounds were soon gone, leaving the artillery crews with only the standard high-explosive shells. After the first wave of eight tanks, more North Korean T-34s followed, coming down the road in groups of four. By 9:00 A.M. a total of thirty-three tanks had rolled past Task Force Smith's infantry position, their fire killing or wounding some twenty U.S. troops. As the tanks approached the U.S. artillery position, they sped up to make a run, one at a time, past the 105mm howitzers. The artillery crews continued firing and disabled three more tanks by hitting them in the tracks. Three others were slightly damaged but were able to continue down the road. By about 10:15 A.M. the last North Korean tank had passed the artillery position.

An eerie silence descended over Task Force Smith. Rain continued to fall on the now empty road to Seoul. But Brad Smith knew that his position would not remain quiet for long; although the tanks were gone, the NKPA infantry would not be far behind.

The NKPA Advances

About an hour after the last North Korean tank had come and gone, Smith once more saw movement on the road. A long column of trucks and soldiers was advancing along the road toward Task Force Smith. From his vantage point at a forward observation post, Smith estimated that the column was six miles long. He could see three tanks at the head of the column, followed by numerous trucks and a line of marching soldiers that extended for miles.

Smith watched for an hour as the column slowly progressed toward the task force's position. Although Smith could not know it at the time, the approaching troops, two regiments of the NKPA's Fourth Division, were experienced, battle-hardened soldiers. MacArthur's "arrogant display of force" now seemed quite insignificant compared to the Communist force with which it was about to do battle.

When the tanks at the head of the column were about a thousand yards from Task Force Smith's position, Smith gave the order to fire, telling his men to "throw the book at them!"[18] Smith's troops raked the enemy column with mortar and machine-gun fire. Some of the North Korean trucks burst into flame, their troops scrambling off the burning vehicles and beginning to return fire. Private Bob Fitzgerald, one of the men of the Fifty-second Field Artillery Battalion assigned to infantry duty, described the scene as the battle unfolded:

They piled out of the trucks, and some came straight across the fields at us while more of them started off to the right and left to get around our flanks. I'm pouring rounds into them now, and I could see some of them dropping in the fields. I could hear bullets zinging past my head, I could see bullets kicking up the dirt in front of me, I could see mortar rounds coming in, exploding on the hill in front and off to the side of me, in

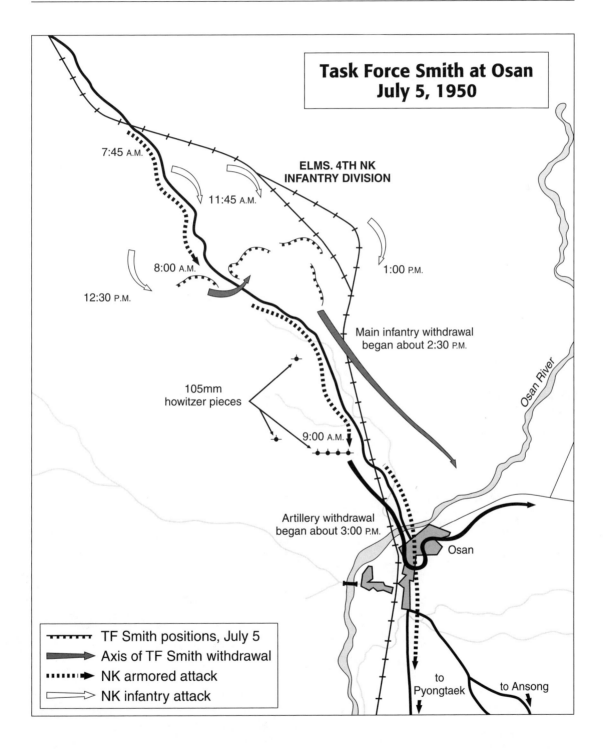

**Task Force Smith at Osan
July 5, 1950**

7:45 A.M.

ELMS. 4TH NK
INFANTRY DIVISION

11:45 A.M.

8:00 A.M.

1:00 P.M.

12:30 P.M.

Main infantry withdrawal
began about 2:30 P.M.

Osan River

105mm
howitzer pieces

9:00 A.M.

Artillery withdrawal
began about 3:00 P.M.

Osan

TF Smith positions, July 5
Axis of TF Smith withdrawal
NK armored attack
NK infantry attack

to
Pyongtaek

to Ansong

among our positions. They got us zeroed in a hurry, and they were pouring a hell of a lot of fire into us.[19]

While the North Korean tanks were firing on the U.S. position, about a thousand of the enemy began to spread out. U.S. fire prevented the North Koreans from advancing directly up the road, so they began moving up the ridge on the east side of the road. Soon enemy troops began to appear on a hill on the west side of the road; the NKPA troops were trying to encircle Task Force Smith. With their ammunition dwindling, U.S. troops continued to pour mortar, machine-gun, and rifle fire onto the

Two South Korean soldiers load an antitank gun to stop the advance of North Korean T-34 tanks. Such tanks gave the Communist forces an advantage during the war's early stages.

enemy. But the North Koreans kept advancing south, and by 2:30 on the afternoon of July 5 it appeared inevitable that they would eventually surround Task Force Smith. It was, as Smith later recalled, "an obviously hopeless situation, with many casualties, no communications, no transportation, ammo gone, and the enemy tanks now well behind me."[20] Smith now had a difficult decision to make. "To stand and die, or try to get the remains of my task force out of there? I could last, at best, only another hour, and then lose everything I had. I chose to try to get out, in hopes that we would live to fight another day."[21] His decision made, Brad Smith had no way of knowing that the retreat would result in the heaviest casualties for Task Force Smith.

Retreat

Smith's plan for withdrawal called for leapfrogging his men, with each departing unit being protected by the unit ahead of it. As the retreat began, the enemy intensified its attack on the task force. "Enemy fire got worse," recalled a lieutenant, "especially on the flanks. . . . When we moved out we began taking more and more casualties. . . . Guys fell around me. Mortar rounds hit here and there."[22] Task Force Smith headed toward Osan, moving south along the western side of the railroad tracks. The men carried only their personal weapons; all larger weapons, such as mortars, recoilless rifles, and machine guns were abandoned to the enemy. Tragically, the Americans also had

to leave behind their dead comrades and some twenty-five to thirty wounded. "You read a lot about the wounded litter cases being left behind," recalled Bob Roy. "But I saw guys who should've gotten medals. I saw guys carrying other guys who had been shot in the legs. There were a lot of guys trying to help other people out."[23] Those wounded who were able to walk joined the retreat, but as enemy fire increased many of them fell behind and were not seen again.

As the infantry withdrew, Smith made his way to the artillery position, expecting to find all the artillery pieces destroyed and the crews dead. He discovered, however, that the howitzers were undamaged and only two men wounded. After removing the sights and breech locks from the guns to make them inoperable, the artillerymen headed south, picking up their trucks near Osan where they had left them. Finding some enemy tanks in Osan, Smith and the artillery convoy headed east on a small dirt road that, he hoped, would take them to safety in the town of Ansong. Along the way they picked up stragglers from the task force who were trudging south through the rice paddies; many of them had lost their helmets, shirts, and even boots. About one hundred exhausted soldiers joined the convoy, which reached Ansong by nightfall.

After spending the night at Ansong, what was left of Task Force Smith moved on to Chonan, farther southeast along the line of retreat. There, Lieutenant Colonel

Smith was able to assess the condition of his task force. Out of his original force of more than 500 men, Smith counted 185 survivors at Chonan. Later 65 more arrived, bringing the total to 250. Over the next few days other survivors showed up at Chonan and at various other towns. Twelve men from Company B reached Chonan on July 7 after encountering five North Korean roadblocks. A few stragglers even walked all the way to the Yellow Sea and the Sea of Japan.

Aftermath

For Task Force Smith, the Battle of Osan was an impossible fight against an overwhelming foe. "No More Task Force Smiths" became a rallying cry against hastily throwing

Retreat of a "Me-Gook"

Lieutenant William Wyrick, platoon leader of C Company, Twenty-first Infantry, recalls the experience of retreating after the destruction of Task Force Smith in *The Korean War: Pusan to Chosin: An Oral History* by Donald Knox:

> We had crossed the mountains by following trails, but now we moved south on the dirt road running down the middle of the valley. It must have been 7:00 or 8:00 P.M., although it was still good daylight. I don't remember any rain after crossing the first ridge east of the railroad. We had little or nothing to eat as all rations had been consumed or thrown away earlier during the day. Some men would run out into the fields on either side of the road to dig vegetables to eat. We were not physically able to stop them, and once they left the road they didn't respond to our orders to return. I know some of them did return to the column after finding some food. . . . We continued to move, stopping only for breaks every thirty or forty minutes. We were exhausted and it was very difficult to get everyone up and moving again as most were falling asleep during the ten-to-fifteen-minute breaks. It was awfully hot in Korea in July. We were out of treated water and were drinking out of the rice paddies. By

the time it grew dark (9:00 to 10:00 P.M.), we were completely exhausted and were stopping for breaks more frequently. . . .

Wyrick became separated from his group and had to continue his journey alone. He soon saw a village off to the left of the road:

> Just before I reached the edge of the village, I heard a challenge in Korean. (I knew three Korean words at the time. On the way north someone had told us that "me-gook" meant "American," that "ee-da-wa" meant "come here," and "ka-da" meant "get away.") I responded "me-gook" and the guy, a Korean policeman, didn't shoot at me. He let me approach and use his telephone to call the police station in the center of town. I discovered that my group . . . [was] already at the police station. Someone then took me there. . . . I had a hot cup of coffee and something (probably rice) to eat. Then I made a mistake; I took off my wet boots and went to sleep. About an hour later, around 6:00 A.M., someone shouted that the North Koreans were approaching the north edge of town. I had a very difficult time getting my boots on; in fact, I thought for a while I was going to go barefoot.

inexperienced and underequipped soldiers into combat. Considering the odds against Smith's force, the final tally of 20 killed and 130 wounded could have been much worse. Yet Task Force Smith failed to stop the on-rushing NKPA as it swept down the Korean peninsula toward the southern port city of Pusan. "We were sent over there to delay the North Koreans," said Private Bob Roy, who survived the Battle of Osan. "We delayed them seven hours. Don't ask me if it was worth it. We were a bunch of kids and we were just trying to do our jobs."[24]

To the timorous ROK army and its in-experienced U.S. comrades, the NKPA must have seemed a nearly invincible force. But soon the leader of the United Nations Command would propose a dar-ing scheme that, if successful, might just turn the war around.

Chapter 3

The Landing at Inchon

By the late summer of 1950, the North Korean People's Army (NKPA) had marched down the Korean peninsula unhindered by either the Republic of Korea (ROK) army or the United Nations (UN) forces sent to delay the Communist advance. Now the defenders were making a last stand around the port of Pusan, South Korea, and the NKPA was poised to drive them into the sea. A plan was needed to prevent the NKPA from overrunning the entire peninsula, and it was needed quickly.

A Bold Plan

On August 23, 1950, a group of high-ranking U.S. military officials were seated in a room on the sixth floor of the Dai Ichi Building in Tokyo, Japan. They were assembled to hear the details of a plan for an amphibious invasion of Korea at Inchon, a port city on the west coast. The plan was the brainchild of General Douglas MacArthur, who had prepared and exe-

cuted numerous successful amphibious landings in the Pacific during World War II. But before he spoke, the discussion centered on the difficulties of landing at Inchon.

Inchon was a strategic place for an invasion, being deep behind enemy lines and only about twenty miles from South Korea's capital, Seoul. But to many of the officers at that meeting, Inchon was the worst place for an amphibious assault. Lieutenant Commander Arlie Capps, a gunnery officer, recalled, "We drew up a list of every natural and geographic handicap —and Inchon had 'em all."[25] Inchon's tides varied by some thirty-two feet, so only a few days each month were suitable for a landing. At low tide, mudflats covered the shoreline, creating the danger of landing craft getting stranded. Even at high tide, the sea level remained several feet below the beaches; the invading forces would have to scale high rock seawalls before they could press their attack. Swift currents

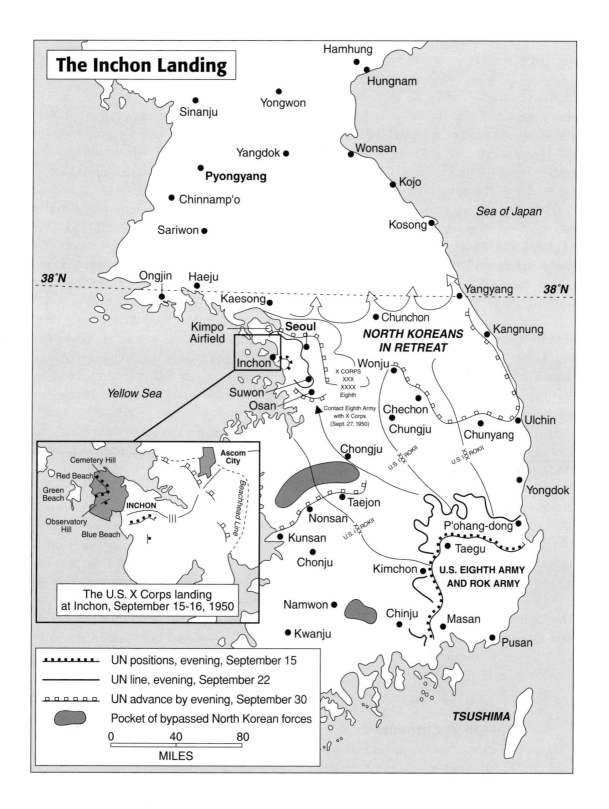

The Inchon Landing

Hamhung

Hungnam

Sinanju

Yongwon

Wonsan

Yangdok

Kojo

Pyongyang

Chinnamp'o

Kosong

Sariwon

Sea of Japan

38°N

Ongjin

Haeju

Yangyang

38°N

Kaesong

Chunchon

Kangnung

Kimpo Airfield

Seoul

Yellow Sea

Inchon

NORTH KOREANS IN RETREAT

Wonju

X CORPS
XXX
XXXX
Eighth

Suwon

Osan

Chechon

Ulchin

Contact Eighth Army
with X Corps
(Sept. 27, 1950)

Chungju

Chunyang

U.S. X

ROK II

U.S. I

ROK II

Chongju

Ascom
City

Cemetery Hill

Red Beach

Green
Beach

INCHON

Beachhead Line

Yongdok

Taejon

Observatory
Hill

Blue Beach

Nonsan

U.S. IX

ROK II

P'ohang-dong

Kunsan

Taegu

Chonju

The U.S. X Corps landing
at Inchon, September 15-16, 1950

Kimchon

**U.S. EIGHTH ARMY
AND ROK ARMY**

Namwon

Chinju

Masan

Kwanju

Pusan

········ UN positions, evening, September 15

———— UN line, evening, September 22

▫▫▫▫▫ UN advance by evening, September 30

    Pocket of bypassed North Korean forces

TSUSHIMA

0   40   80

MILES

in the channels leading to Inchon were also a problem, and the height of the typhoon season was fast approaching. Admiral James Doyle, who would eventually lead the amphibious assault, summed up his feelings: "The operation is not impossible, but I do not recommend it."[26]

After all the objections had been heard, it was MacArthur's turn. In an eloquent yet conversational speech, the general presented his case for the Inchon landing. "The enemy, I am convinced," said MacArthur, "has failed to prepare Inchon properly for defense. The very arguments you have made as to the impracticabilities involved will tend to ensure for me the element of surprise. . . . [The] seizure of Inchon and Seoul will cut the enemy's supply line and seal off the entire southern peninsula. The vulnerability of the enemy is his supply position." After forty-five minutes, MacArthur quietly concluded his remarks: "I can almost hear the ticking of the second hand of destiny. We must act now or we will die. . . . Inchon will not fail. Inchon will succeed. And it will save 100,000 lives."[27]

The room on the sixth floor of the Dai Ichi Building remained hushed. MacArthur had made his case. Five days later he received official permission from Washington to prepare for and execute his daring plan.

Operation Chromite

The amphibious invasion of Inchon was given the code name Operation Chromite, and it was scheduled to take place on September 15, 1950. The plan called for navy ships and marine and navy aircraft to soften up the landing site with a two-day bombardment of Wolmi-do, a fortified island guarding the mouth of Inchon's harbor. After the bombardment, U.S. Marines would put ashore on the island at an area designated Green Beach to eliminate any remaining North Korean resistance. Then, a larger force of soldiers and marines would invade Inchon itself, landing at two areas designated Red Beach and Blue Beach. Their mission was to secure the port and prepare it for the tanks, trucks, and additional troops that would follow. With Inchon in UN hands, the troops would next capture nearby Kimpo airfield, then move on toward Seoul, about twenty miles to the east, and prepare to cut off the NKPA.

The actual landing at Inchon would be carried out by the newly activated X (Tenth) Corps. Commanded by General Edward Almond, X Corps was made up of the First Marine Division and the Seventh Army Division, along with supporting artillery, antiaircraft, and engineer units. Each division also included troops from the ROK army and marines. In all, some 230 ships and 70,000 troops would take part in the invasion.

Shortly after midnight on September 13, MacArthur boarded the USS *Mount McKinley* in the port of Sasebo, Japan. The vessel would serve as the command ship for the general and his top officers

during the assault on Inchon. As the ship headed out to sea, MacArthur contemplated the impending invasion: "I had made many landings before," he recalled, "but this was the most intricately complicated amphibious operation I had ever attempted."[28]

Assault on Wolmi-do

Operation Chromite had actually begun even before MacArthur stepped aboard the *Mount McKinley*. On September 10 navy and marine aircraft began a series of assaults against the island of Wolmi-do ("Moon Tip Island"). Marine Corsairs dropped ninety-five thousand pounds of

U.S. Marines lead a patrol on Wolmi-do Island. Capturing Wolmi-do was integral to the UN's invasion at Inchon harbor.

napalm, a form of highly flammable jellied gasoline, setting fire to the island. The naval bombardment began on September 13, when a column of five destroyers and four cruisers entered Flying Fish Channel, the narrow sea-lane leading to Inchon. Shortly after noon the ships began their heavy shelling of Wolmi-do. The North Korean defenders on the island, estimated by intelligence reports as about four hundred soldiers, returned fire with 75mm artillery pieces dug into protective emplacements. "A necklace of gun-flashes sparkled around the waist of the island," wrote an Associated Press reporter. "The flashes were reddish-gold and they came so fast that soon the entire slope was sparkling with pinpoints of fire."[29] For two days the ships pounded Wolmi-do and shelled Inchon on the mainland. Finally, the guns of Wolmi-do fell silent. A pilot flying over the once-wooded island remarked that it "looked like it had been shaved."[30]

The invasion would be a two-stage operation, with the timing of each stage dictated by the tides. The high tides necessary for the landing on September 15 would occur at 6:59 A.M. and 7:19 P.M. Just before 6:00 A.M. marines of the Third Battalion, Fifth Regiment began climbing into seventeen boats called LCVPs (land-

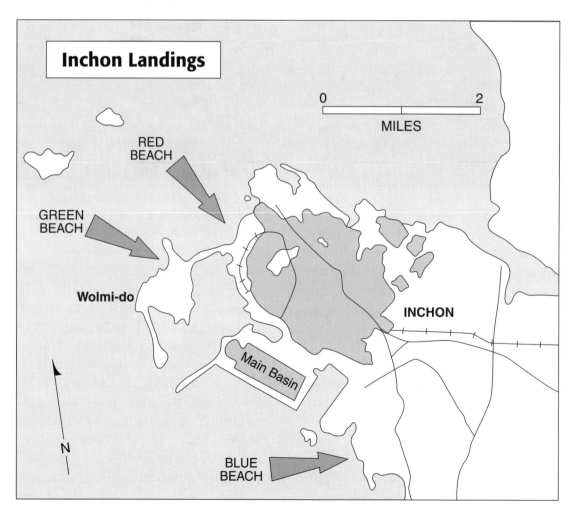

Inchon Landings

RED
BEACH

GREEN
BEACH

Wolmi-do

Main Basin

INCHON

BLUE
BEACH

0   2

MILES

N

Beacon for an Invasion

As General Douglas MacArthur gazed through his binoculars at the shoreline of Inchon before the landing, he spied a lighthouse on the small island of Palmi-do, its light shining brightly. Previously out of order, that lighthouse had been activated by a U.S. naval officer in one of the most daring covert operations of the Korean War.

Two weeks before the invasion, MacArthur lacked vital, detailed information about the physical characteristics of the area his force was about to invade. To provide this information, he called on Eugene Clark, a thirty-nine-year-old navy lieutenant in the general's intelligence office in Tokyo. With two South Korean officers, Clark secretly landed on the island of Yonghung-do in Inchon harbor. The small contingent of spies then went about collecting information about Inchon's treacherous tides, mudflats, and high seawalls. One goal of Clark's mission was to get an old lighthouse on Palmi-do Island in Flying Fish Channel working to guide the invasion force. In his book, *The Secrets of Inchon: The Untold Story of the Most Daring Covert Mission of the Korean War,* Clark relates his actions, and doubts, on September 15, 1950, the day of the Inchon invasion:

> It was 0030 [12:30 A.M.] on the fifteenth when we landed on Palmi-do. The light should be in operation right now. We'd promised it. The fleet, twenty miles down the channel, would be starting through without a light, thinking we had failed. We

started running and were caught up short by a machine-gun burst at our feet and hit the ground instinctively. . . . By the time we arrived at the top, my heart was beating like a trip-hammer and I could barely hoist myself up the steel-runged ladder to the light. It was 0050 [12:50 A.M.] when we adjusted the vector shade to throw the light down Flying Fish Channel. I felt defeated. Everything had gone wrong at the last. Good planning would have avoided all this. I opened the small hatch that led out onto the narrow catwalk outside the light and went out.

But the plan had not failed. Before long, Clark saw shadows in the water some two hundred feet below the lighthouse's catwalk.

> It was the invasion force. Silently, ghostly, six dark shapes, lean and hungry from this vantage point, were gliding by beneath us. It was like a dream or a nightmare. I knew those ships. Had served in them. How could they move without noise? But they did. If it weren't for my eyes, I wouldn't believe them to be there.

> Slowly, they slid out of sight around the eastern tip of Palmi-do, and their places were taken by others and still others. Finally, the huge shapes of the cruisers loomed up and took their stations. This was the day. This was it.

ing craft, vehicles, and personnel). These squat, thirty-six-foot-long vessels could each hold more than thirty-five men and had a ramp at the bow that would be lowered to discharge the assault troops. Larger landing craft, one-hundred-twenty-foot-long LSUs (landing ship, utility), would carry tanks and more troops to the beach.

At a signal from the command ship *Mount McKinley,* the landing craft revved their engines and headed for Wolmi-do.

Guns from the naval vessels were once more shelling the island, and this time the attack included rockets launched from three "rocket ships" anchored in the channel. Aircraft screamed low overhead, launching rockets, dropping bombs, and raking the island with machine-gun fire. "The roar of their engines," recalled Private First Class Fred Davidson, "hit us like a bomb. Those marine Corsairs came flying through the smoke toward the beach not thirty feet over our heads! Hot, empty machine-gun shells fell on us. Talk about close air support."[31] Smoke enveloped Wolmi-do, making the demarcation between land and water indistinguishable. So devastating was the bombardment that a marine aboard one of the LCVPs shouted, "Save us a little of that island!"[32] At 6:29 the barrage ended as the landing craft neared Wolmi-do; it was time for the invasion to begin.

Green Beach

The first wave of LCVPs hit the beach at Wolmi-do at 6:33 A.M. on September 15, 1950. The bow ramps of the landing craft were lowered, and the marines dashed onto Green Beach with guns aimed. A few minutes later the second wave of marines hit the beach, ready to repel any North Korean resistance that had survived the preinvasion bombardment. But what confronted them was a shattered landscape. "As soon as I hit the beach," recalled Davidson, "I turned to my right. . . . It was hard to see because of all the smoke. All the trees I passed had been blown down."[33] Other than some scattered rifle fire, there was little opposition to the marines on Green Beach, and the island's surviving defenders soon surrendered. Frank Gibney, a correspondent for *Time* magazine, was with the marines on Wolmi-do:

> As I dashed up the slope of the beach, I got my first look at Wolmi Island's

Landing craft carrying U.S. troops head for Blue Beach during Operation Chromite. A total of seventy thousand UN soldiers landed at Inchon.

defenders. Three or four half-naked North Korean soldiers, hands held rigid over their pinched, scared faces, stumbled into one of their old shallow trenches at the command of a marine. I talked to them in Japanese. "Are you going to kill us?" stammered one. When I said we wouldn't, he chattered to the others and a little of the fear went out of their eyes.[34]

Other North Korean soldiers who had holed up in caves on the island were forced out by hand grenades tossed into their hiding places. In all, 136 North Korean prisoners were captured in the assault on Wolmi-do.

One of the main objectives was the capture of Radio Hill, the highest point on the island, which looked down on all the invasion beaches. The marines moved off Green Beach and started up the slope toward the peak of the hill. Encountering no resistance, they wasted no time in securing the 351-foot-tall rise. "We got to the top of Radio Hill," recalled Private First Class Jack Wright, "and found a great big bowllike depression. . . . All of a sudden, everyone, everything, just went quiet. Standing there, looking around, it hit us all at once. The island was ours. We'd taken it!"[35] One-half hour after the invasion of Wolmi-do began, an American flag was flying over Radio Hill.

The marines destroyed several caves where NKPA troops who refused to surrender were hiding and took control of a narrow causeway connecting Wolmi-do with the mainland. At 8:00 A.M. a message was sent to the *Mount McKinley* that the island was secure. The first phase of Operation Chromite had succeeded with only seventeen marines wounded and none killed. One hundred eight North Korean soldiers had been killed and perhaps a hundred more buried in the rubble of demolished caves. General MacArthur had watched the assault through binoculars as he sat in a swivel chair on the bridge of the *Mount McKinley*, surrounded by his senior officers. MacArthur recalled his reaction when word came that Wolmi-do was in UN hands with few casualties: "I turned to Admiral Doyle and said: Please send this message to the fleet: 'The Navy and the Marines have never shone more brightly than this morning.'"[36] Then the general turned to his comrades on the bridge and said, "That's it. Let's get a cup of coffee."[37]

As the tides receded around Wolmi-do and Inchon, the invasion fleet pulled back to avoid being left aground on the mudflats. All MacArthur and his troops could do now was to wait for the evening's high tide to launch the next phase of Operation Chromite.

Assault on Inchon

The invasion of the mainland would take place at two positions: Red Beach, an area that fronted Inchon's industrial district north of Wolmi-do, and Blue Beach, to the south of the city. As with the morning's assault on Wolmi-do, prior to the invasion the landing areas would be softened up by fire from the operation's ships. At 2:30 on the afternoon of September 15, the naval bombardment began. Soon marines were climbing into their landing craft, ready to begin the assault. James Bell, a correspondent for *Time* magazine, described the scene:

> The dirty yellow waters of Inchon harbor bore a tremendous array of boats. As far as the eye could see there were LCVPs in groups of five making endless circles before the great grey assault ships. Ahead were the cruisers, destroyers and rocket ships. Overhead, Navy and Marine planes streaked for targets ashore. The big guns boomed like tremendous bass drums. The smaller 40-mm. guns hammered away with the incessant roll of snare drums.[38]

After the big guns ceased their barrage, the rocket ships took over. So furious was their fire that six thousand rockets burst onto Inchon in just twenty minutes. A haze of smoke, hanging over the landing beaches and mixed with a steadily falling drizzle, made for poor visibility. But the landing craft and their cargo of marines made their way slowly toward the seawalls that protected the beaches. Bobbing in the water alongside them were amphibious tractors (amtracs) for crawling over the muddy beaches. "Get 'em ready," said a company commander to his sergeant in one of the landing craft. Then he gave his

men final instructions. "There's a ditch on the other side of the wall. Roll over the wall into the ditch, then get up fast and make for the right side of the beach. Good luck to all of you."[39]

At 5:33 P.M. the first landing craft hit the wall at Red Beach.

Red Beach

With revving engines holding their LCVPs against the wall, men of the Fifth Marine Regiment began lobbing grenades over the seawall at an enemy they could not yet see. "Up and over!"[40] yelled a lieutenant, and marines began to clamber up makeshift wooden and aluminum ladders placed against the rock wall. Some of them were immediately cut down as NKPA machine-gun fire from protective bunkers and rifle fire from enemy soldiers beyond the beach raked the top of the seawall. Most of the marines made it over, however, and began advancing into Inchon, killing or capturing North Korean soldiers as they encountered them. The defenders put up a stiff resistance, killing eight marines and wounding twenty-eight.

Confusion plagued the operation as more marines hit Red Beach. The smoke and approaching darkness hampered visibility. Mistakes were made as everyone hurried to get the invasion force landed before the tide went out. Some LCVPs delivered their troops to the wrong spots on the beach. Commanders had a difficult time rounding up their own troops in the mass

Picture of a Hero

While capturing the images of a war, combat photographers often take pictures that turn out to have historic significance. The famous World War II photo of marines raising the U.S. flag on Mount Suribachi is a familiar and dramatic image. In Donald Knox's *The Korean War: Pusan to Chosin: An Oral History*, Lieutenant Tom Gibson describes another such photograph, this one of a Korean War hero:

> There's a famous photograph of the Marines landing on Red Beach. Taken from the rear of an LCVP, it shows a lot of Marines waiting to climb over the seawall. One Marine, however, is already on a ladder. His right leg is on the seawall, his right arm, in which he's holding his rifle, is steadying him on the ramp, his back is hunched. That Marine is [Baldomero] Punchy Lopez.
>
> Moments later he took out a North Korean bunker. A second bunker remained. Lopez began to attack it. Before he could throw the grenade he held in his hand he was hit. The gre-

nade dropped to his side. To save the men of his platoon he rolled over on top of it.

First Lieutenant Baldomero Lopez was twenty-five-years old when he gave his life to save his fellow marines. For his heroic action, he was posthumously awarded the Medal of Honor.

First Lieutenant Baldomero Lopez scales the seawall at Inchon's Red Beach.

of men now on the beach. When LSTs (landing ship, tank) began arriving at the seawall, some mistakenly began firing into areas already occupied by marines. But despite these problems, the invasion continued with relatively little opposition.

A little more than twenty minutes after hitting Red Beach, the marines had

pushed into Inchon and seized Cemetery Hill, one of their first objectives. Two other knolls, Observatory Hill and British Consulate Hill, both held enemy soldiers who fired down on Red Beach from their elevated vantage points. After fighting against scattered NKPA resistance, marines took control of British Consulate Hill around 6:45 P.M., and by midnight they had secured Observatory Hill.

Blue Beach

While the Fifth Marines were assaulting Red Beach, four miles away landing craft carrying the First Marine Regiment were hitting the seawalls on Blue Beach. The First Marines had actually landed at Blue Beach one minute before the Fifth Marines landed at Red Beach. The first three waves

of landing craft hit their intended targets at the Blue Beach seawall, sending their marines over the top or through holes blasted in the wall. But because of the increasing smoke and rain, subsequent waves had trouble finding their correct landing area. One marine major, concerned that the craft in which he was riding was off course, asked the pilot if he had a compass. "Search me," the recently recruited sailor replied. "Six weeks ago I was driving a truck

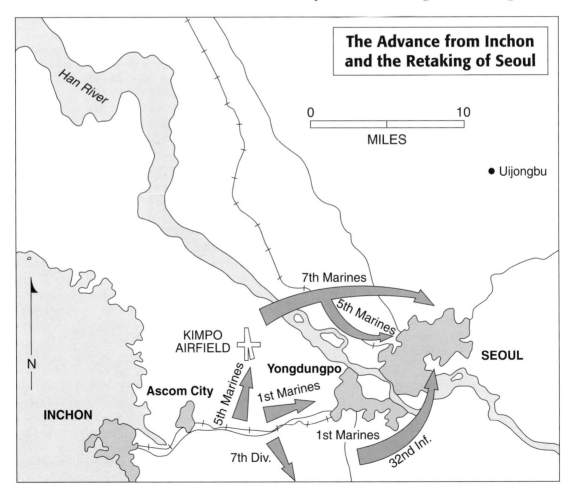

Marguerite Higgins, War Correspondent

Of the numerous newspaper and magazine reporters to cover the combat operations of the Korean War, only one was a woman. Marguerite Higgins was born in Hong Kong in 1920. She studied journalism at the University of California and at Columbia University in New York. Higgins began her journalism career with a part-time job at the *New York Herald Tribune* and became a war correspondent at the end of World War II. When the Korean War broke out, Higgins was the *Tribune*'s bureau chief in Tokyo, Japan. Within days of the North Korean invasion, she was at the front in Korea.

In September 1950, Marguerite Higgins and two other reporters hit the beach with the marines at Inchon. The following excerpt is from her book *War in Korea: The Report of a Woman Combat Correspondent:*

The control ship signaled that it was our turn.

"Here we go—keep your heads down," shouted Lieutenant Shening.

As we rushed toward the sea wall an amber-colored star shell burst above the beach. It meant that our first objective, the cemetery, had been taken. But before we could even begin to relax, brightly colored tracer bullets cut across our bow and across the open top of our boat. I heard the authoritative rattle of machine guns. Some-

how the enemy had survived the terrible pounding they'd been getting. No matter what had happened to the first four waves, the Reds had sighted us and their aim was excellent. . . . Then our boat smashed hard into a dip in the seawall.

"Come on, you big, brave marines—let's get the hell out of here," yelled Lieutenant Shening, emphasizing his words with good, hard shoves. The photographer announced that he had had enough and was going straight back to the transport. For a second I was tempted to go with him. Then a new burst of fire made me decide to get out of the boat fast. I maneuvered my typewriter into a position where I could reach it once I had dropped over the side. I got a footing on the steel ledge on the side of the boat and pushed myself over. I landed in about three feet of water in the dip of the sea wall.

A warning burst, probably a grenade, forced us all down, and we snaked along on our stomachs over the boulders to a sort of curve below the top of the dip. It gave us a cover of sorts from the tracer bullets, and we three newsmen and most of the marines flattened out and waited there. As we waited, wave after wave of marines hit the beach, and soon there must have been sixty or more of us lying on our bellies in the small dip.

in San Francisco."[41] Some of the amtracs used in the assault on Blue Beach were pressed into service so quickly that they did not even have radios; many got bogged down in the mud.

Still, the assault on Blue Beach went more smoothly than the landing on Red Beach. Marines moved out and occupied

several hills, forcing the NKPA defenders to flee. They knocked out a tower concealing a machine-gun nest some five hundred yards from the beach. Circling around to the east of Inchon, the marines seized a hill after killing fifty North Korean troops and capturing fifteen. Gradually all resistance ceased and Inchon became quiet.

The initial objective of Operation Chromite had been achieved at a cost of 20 marines killed, 1 missing in action, and 174 wounded. The North Koreans suffered 1,350 casualties out of a defending force of some 2,000 NKPA troops. Thirteen thousand marines, plus tanks, jeeps, trucks, and other heavy equipment, had come ashore on the beaches of Inchon.

On to Seoul

With Inchon secure, on September 16, 1950, the marines began moving east toward Seoul. MacArthur's goal was to retake the South Korean capital by September 25—three months to the day since the North Korean invasion began. On September 18, marines seized Kimpo airfield, opening it for UN combat support aircraft and cargo planes that would bring in supplies and ammunition. The NKPA hurriedly diverted units to try to stop the UN push to Seoul, but the Communist force was no match for MacArthur's troops. Although the North Koreans put

up a fierce struggle, by September 25, MacArthur's deadline, the marines had entered Seoul. The next day MacArthur announced that Seoul had been recaptured, but the city was not yet secure. Bitter fighting continued in the streets of the capital for two more days until the NKPA was finally routed. Operation Chromite was over.

In an official ceremony on September 29, 1950, MacArthur returned Seoul to President Syngman Rhee. "In behalf of the United Nations Command," MacArthur told Rhee, "I am happy to restore to you, Mr. President, the seat of your government that from it you may better fulfill your constitutional responsibilities."[42] With the South Korean flag flying again over Seoul, no one could foresee that the capital was destined to fall once more into the hands of Communist troops.

Two hundred miles south of Inchon, UN forces were desperately defending the last small piece of real estate they held in South Korea: the Pusan Perimeter.

Chapter 4

Defending the Pusan Perimeter

After crossing the 38th parallel on June 25, 1950, the Communist North Korean People's Army (NKPA) marched steadily south across the rivers, hills, and rice paddies of South Korea. Along the way these well-trained and experienced troops, fortified with Russian-made tanks, pushed back the South Korean and U.S. soldiers who had been hastily deployed to stop them. By late summer it seemed that nothing could stop the NKPA from occupying the entire peninsula and, thus, bringing the Republic of Korea (ROK) into the Communist fold.

Pusan, a vital port city on the southeastern tip of South Korea, was the end of the line for the U.S. and ROK troops. Further withdrawal would be impossible, for beyond Pusan lay nothing but the Korea Strait and certain defeat. As the soldiers began setting up a defensive perimeter around Pusan, they knew they would have to defend it at all costs.

An Invincible Foe?

Within two days of the North Korean invasion, the NKPA was beating back the ROK forces south of the 38th parallel. Despite a valiant effort to delay the enemy's advance, the ROK troops were simply no match for the North Korean tanks. When Seoul, the capital of the Republic of Korea, fell to the NKPA on June 27, President Syngman Rhee and his officials fled ninety miles south to Taejon, where they set up a new seat of government. By July 19, 1950, the North Korean advance was nearing Taejon. In two days of bloody battle, the NKPA surrounded the ROK and two regiments of the Twenty-fourth Division. Unable to hold the town, what remained of the United Nations (UN) forces finally retreated, suffering a total of 1,150 killed, wounded, or missing in action. Several days later troops from the Twenty-ninth Regiment were ambushed near the town of Chinju, losing 313 killed and 100 captured. It was

the second-worst loss of U.S. troops in a single battle of the Korean War.

It seemed as if nothing could stop the North Koreans. As Uzal Ent, a young American lieutenant, recalled, "It seemed like we were continually falling back, and there was no indication where it would end. There was a real fear that we'd be pushed right out of Korea."[43] World opinion seemed to agree. "Enough of this nonsense," complained a British newspaper. "The United States should recognize a lost cause and stop pouring men into this Asian sinkhole." A smug Soviet Union ridiculed the "futile attempts of the American imperialists to halt the aspirations of the Korean peoples for unity, indepen-

General Walton Harris Walker (right) arrives in Korea in July 1950. MacArthur gave General Walker command of all U.S. forces in Korea.

dence and freedom."[44] Of course, unity from the Soviet point of view meant uniting Korea under communism. The job of preventing that outcome would fall to one man: General Walton H. Walker, commander of the Eighth U.S. Army in Korea.

"Stand or Die"

General Walton Harris Walker graduated from the U.S. Military Academy at West Point in 1912. A decorated company commander in World War I, he led an armored corps in World War II and was promoted to lieutenant general at the end of that conflict. When the Korean War began, Walker was commander of the Eighth U.S. Army, an element of General Douglas MacArthur's Far East Command in Japan. Due to a reduction in military spending after World War II, the Eighth Army's four divisions—the Seventh, Twenty-fourth, and Twenty-fifth Infantry and the First Cavalry (also infantry, despite the name)—were poorly equipped and undermanned. In addition, very few of the soldiers had any real combat experience. That these troops were no match for the battle-hardened NKPA became clear with the defeat of Task Force Smith, an element of the Twenty-fourth Division.

On July 12, 1950, the Eighth U.S. Army in Korea (EUSAK) officially became responsible for all ground operations in Korea. Upon receiving orders from General MacArthur, Walker assumed command of all U.S. forces in Korea. The next day he arrived at his headquarters at Taegu, about sixty miles north of the port of Pusan. As the month of July wore on and the North Koreans pushed farther south, more U.S. soldiers arrived in Korea. Walker visited his units and flew over the battlefield in an observation plane to get a firsthand look at the situation. Despite heavy losses and forced withdrawals, many of his units were bravely fighting against the overwhelming Communist assault. In addition, more troops and desperately needed equipment such as tanks and artillery were beginning to arrive at Pusan.

Recalling the World War II Battle of the Bulge, in which U.S. troops initially retreated only to regroup and ultimately defeat the German enemy, Walker felt that his men could do the same.

On July 29, Walker told his staff that further retreat would not be tolerated:

> We are fighting a battle against time. There will be no retreating, withdrawal, or readjustments of the lines or any other term you choose. There is no line behind us to which we can retreat. Every unit must counterattack to keep the enemy in a state of confusion and off balance. . . . We must fight until the end. Capture by these people is worse than death itself. We will fight as a team. If some of us must die, we will die fighting together. Any man who gives ground may be personally responsible for the death of thousands of his comrades. I want you to put this out to all the men in the division. I want everybody to understand that we are going to hold this line. We are going to win.[45]

When Walker's "Stand or Die" order (as it was dubbed by the press) was passed down to the soldiers on the front lines, many of the battle-weary men were not impressed. "Fight to the death?" commented one sergeant. "What does he think we've been doing for a month?"[46] Nevertheless, Walker had his plan figured out, and the line his troops would hold at all costs was called the Pusan Perimeter.

Retreat to the Perimeter

The Pusan Perimeter was roughly rectangular, about fifty miles wide and one hundred miles long, encompassing the southeastern tip of Korea. Rugged mountains formed the perimeter's northern boundary, while the Sea of Japan and the Korea Strait bounded the area on the east and south. The most vulnerable line of the perimeter was the western border,

American infantrymen arrive in Taejon. U.S. troops established their base of operations in Taegu, within the Pusan Perimeter.

which for most of its length was formed by the Naktong River. Within the perimeter was the city of Taegu, which held the headquarters of both the EUSAK and the South Korean government, the latter having abandoned Taejon as the NKPA approached. The perimeter also contained

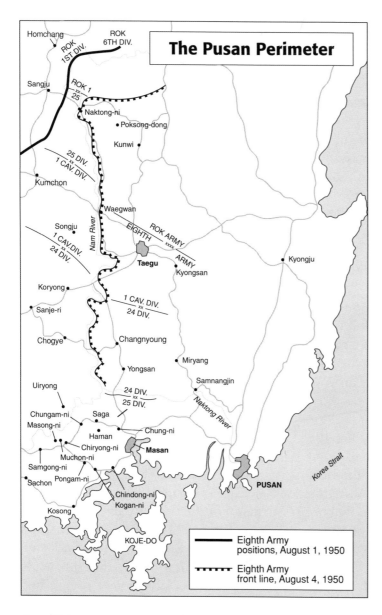

The Pusan Perimeter

Homchang
ROK 1ST DIV.
ROK 6TH DIV.
Sangju
ROK 1
25
Naktong-ni
Poksong-dong
Kunwi
25 DIV.
1 CAV. DIV.
Kumchon
Waegwan
Songju
1 CAV. DIV.
24 DIV.
Nam River
EIGHTH
ROK ARMY
ARMY
Taegu
Kyongsan
Kyongju
Koryong
1 CAV. DIV.
24 DIV.
Sanje-ri
Chogye
Changnyoung
Miryang
Yongsan
Samnangjin
Uiryong
24 DIV.
25 DIV.
Naktong River
Chungam-ni
Saga
Masong-ni
Chung-ni
Haman
Chiryong-ni
Masan
Muchon-ni
Samgong-ni
Pongam-ni
Sachon
Chindong-ni
Kogan-ni
PUSAN
Korea Strait
Kosong
KOJE-DO

—— Eighth Army positions, August 1, 1950

▪▪▪▪ Eighth Army front line, August 4, 1950

Despite Walker's order to stand or die, there was still some retreating to be done. The Eighth Army was fighting the NKPA some ten to twenty miles west of the Naktong River. The general hoped that his men could hold on, but they continued to be pushed back. On August 1, Walker ordered all units of the UN forces in Korea to withdraw behind the Naktong to prepare to defend the Pusan Perimeter. As the military moved to the perimeter, however, so did the South Koreans who were fleeing from the invading NKPA. "You have to imagine the chaos," Lieutenant Ent remarked. "All the roads were jammed with civilian refugees. Sometimes it seemed like everybody in the country was trying to go south. . . . And there were South Korean soldiers mixed in with the civilians."[47]

By August 4, UN forces were established behind the Pusan Perimeter. Under Walker's command were the U.S. First Cavalry, Twenty-fourth and Twenty-fifth Infantry Divisions, and the newly arrived Fifth Regimental Combat Team. ROK units in the perimeter included the First,

the all-important port of Pusan. At the borders of this enclosure General Walker's troops would make their stand, for with nowhere else to go, losing the Pusan Perimeter meant losing the war.

Third, Sixth, Eighth, and Capital Divisions. The U.S. units were deployed along the Naktong, while the ROK troops defended the mountainous northern border. Opposing this force were eleven divisions of the NKPA, six of them along the Naktong River and four at the northern border, with an armored division of about forty tanks held in reserve. Although Walker did not know it at the time, the UN combat forces in the Pusan Perimeter actually outnumbered the enemy by some 92,000 to 70,000. In addition, fresh troops and vitally needed tanks and artillery were arriving daily at Pusan.

With his units deployed along the Pusan Perimeter, Walker decided it was time for action. In early August a group called Task Force Kean began the first UN counteroffensive of the Korean War.

Task Force Kean

As the UN forces assembled along the Pusan Perimeter, the NKPA began exerting pressure at several points along the line. The most serious of these threats was at the southern end of the western defensive line, in a corridor between the towns of Masan and Chinju, twenty-seven miles to the west. Walker gave the job of attacking the enemy at this point to Major General William Kean, the commanding officer of the Twenty-fifth Infantry Division. Kean assembled a task force that included two regiments of the Twenty-fifth Division, the Fifth Regimental Combat Team, and the First Provisional Marine Brigade. The marines,

most of them combat veterans of World War II, were a welcome addition to the UN forces in Korea. Kean had about twenty thousand troops under his command, opposing an enemy force estimated at about seventy-five hundred. His job was to stop the NKPA advance and secure an area near a river named Nam.

On the morning of August 7, the army units of Task Force Kean began their assault with the marine contingent not far behind. Immediately problems arose. An army battalion, unfamiliar with the territory, took a wrong turn down a road, leaving a strategic hill commanding the crossroads unprotected. The annual monsoon rains failed to materialize and temperatures soared to 120 degrees. "Guys almost went mad for water," recalled one marine private. "I never felt the kind of heat I felt in Korea. I just burned up. My hands went numb."[48] Heat exhaustion, along with disease and the rugged terrain, felled many U.S. troops.

Soon Task Force Kean was engaged in a heavy, confusing firefight with NKPA troops. For the next five days the soldiers and marines of Task Force Kean battled with the North Korean troops, a back-and-forth struggle in which neither side made much progress. After a week of fighting, the task force was back to the position it had been in when the assault began. Because of this lack of progress, on August 16 Task Force Kean was disbanded and its troops assigned to other areas along the Pusan Perimeter. Although it had not succeeded in its mission of driving the North Koreans from the Masan-Chinju line, it nevertheless had provided combat experience for its troops and, perhaps more importantly, given the UN forces a psychological boost by going on the offensive for the first time.

While Task Force Kean was fighting against the NKPA in the south of the Pusan Perimeter, other battles had bro-ken out along the line. One of these was at a place called the Naktong Bulge.

Battle of the Naktong Bulge

The Naktong River meanders south through the hills and rice paddies of southern Korea. This serpentine path creates pockets of land within the twists and turns of the river. About seven miles north of where the Naktong joins the

Tank Battle

During the Battle of the Naktong Bulge, the North Koreans employed T-34 tanks, a fearsome weapon supplied to the NKPA by the Soviet Union. This excerpt, however, taken from *The Korean War: Pusan to Chosin: An Oral History* by Donald Knox, shows that the tanks were not invulnerable:

It must have been like the slaughter of great beasts wallowing up out of some prehistoric fen. At the aid station, when the word came that the tanks were coming, Don Kennedy, rifleman, with a shell fragment in his shoulder, got up, got his rifle, and walked up the narrow road and over the hill to the forward slope.

"It was after sundown," Kennedy said later, "but there was plenty of light. I watched the bend in the road where it came around the nose of the hill. You could see the dust rising, and then this long, bulb-nosed gun sort of poked around the corner and wavered back and forth, and then the tank came on.

"It came on slow and nothing happened, and then all of a sudden the bazooka men waiting on the slope started throwing those big rockets into its flanks, whoosh-bam, whoosh-bam, and the rockets went into the sides and into the treads and the bogey wheels. It stopped and began to swing right and left, like an elephant swinging its head, but not moving forward, and it was firing all its guns, but it was firing wild.

"But it didn't fire long, for as soon as the rockets hit and the tank stopped, the 75s [75mm recoilless rifles] cut loose, head-on, and where the 75s hit they tore right through."

Second Lieutenant Frank Muetzel picks up the narrative:

"A second T34 moved around the first one just in time to come under fire from one of our Pershing [tanks] that had moved forward into the cut in the road. The idea was to protect the aid station and CP [command post] by physically blocking the road. The second shot from the Pershing blew straight through the T34's turret and put it immediately out of action. A third enemy tank now turned the curve. It came under fire from everyone in sight—M26s, 3.5s, 75-mm recoilless. In a few minutes it was all over. Everyone jumped into the air and cheered as if he was at a football game."

Nam River, it makes a westward loop, enclosing a twenty-square-mile stretch of land. Called the Naktong Bulge, this area was the site of the first major penetration of the Pusan Perimeter by the NKPA.

Just after midnight on August 6, soldiers of the Sixteenth Regiment of the Fourth NKPA Division quietly crossed the Naktong at the bulge, using rafts or wading through the water with their weapons held over their heads. Guarding the perimeter on the east side of the river were units of the Thirty-fourth Regiment, Twenty-fourth Infantry Division. But with a thirty-four-mile front to defend, the U.S. troops were spread thin, unavoidably leaving gaps in the line. It was through these gaps that the North Koreans came. In the ensuing fight with the understrength Twenty-fourth Division, the NKPA soon took up a position on two elevations that dominated the bulge: Cloverleaf Hill and Obong-ni Ridge (which U.S. soldiers came to call No Name Ridge). This posi-

A Futile Bombing Raid

In August 1950, General Douglas MacArthur was concerned that the North Koreans might soon capture the key city of Taegu just inside the Pusan Perimeter. He suspected an enemy troop buildup across the Naktong River opposite Taegu, near the town of Waegwan. In order to thwart the expected assault, MacArthur proposed that the U.S. Air Force conduct a carpet bombing of the area to destroy the troop concentration gathering across the river.

Carpet bombing, used in World War II and again in Vietnam, called for laying down massive numbers of bombs over a defined locale, thus "carpeting" the area with explosives. MacArthur and General George Stratemeyer, commander of the Far East Air Forces, decided that air force B-29s would bomb a twenty-seven-square-mile area where intelligence reports had indicated as many as forty thousand North Korean troops were massing. Stratemeyer ordered twelve squadrons of bombers readied for the mission. Since no one knew exactly where the enemy was, the target area was divided into twelve equal squares, each square serving as a target for one B-29 squadron.

On August 16, 1950, the twelve bomber squadrons, composed of ninety-eight B-29s, flew over their targets, saturating the area with 3,084 five-hundred-pound bombs and 150 thousand-pound bombs. After the bombing, General O'Donnell, head of the Far East Bomber Command, flew over the target area for two hours but could not detect any enemy movement. Mission accomplished?

Perhaps not. Smoke and dust from the bombing made it difficult to assess the results of the attack from the air, and ground patrols sent to the area were driven back by enemy gunfire. But they probably would not have found any casualties anyway. Later information obtained from North Korean prisoners of war showed that the enemy troops had already crossed the Naktong River and were not in the target zone when the bombers flew their mission. Another carpet bombing mission set for August 19 was canceled, and no such mission would be flown in the future without more precise intelligence regarding troop concentrations.

Although no enemies had been killed, the bombing did have a psychological effect on both sides, boosting the morale of the ROK troops while damaging it for the NKPA.

tion commanded a road that led to the town of Miryang on the Pusan-Taegu road. Should Miryang fall, the main UN supply route would be severed.

The North Koreans began building underwater bridges spanning the Naktong River at the bulge. These allowed armor and artillery to move across the river, and, before long, artillery shells were falling in the nearby town of Yongsan. On August 7 reinforcements began arriving to help the Twenty-fourth Division, whose combat strength was now only about 40 percent. For ten days a seesaw battle with the North Korean invaders raged along Cloverleaf Hill and Obong-ni Ridge; one

U.S. soldiers fire at NKPA targets along the Naktong River. The UN victory at Naktong Bulge saved the vital supply line from Pusan to Taegu.

side would capture the hills, only to lose them to the enemy, and then the process would begin all over again. Although the NKPA was being slowly worn down, the outlook for the Twenty-fourth Division was still not very good. Things would change, however, when the U.S. Marines joined the fight.

Enter the Marines

On the morning of August 17, the First Provisional Marine Brigade attacked enemy positions on Obong-ni Ridge. The assault was preceded by artillery and air attacks on and behind the ridge. The marines advanced on the ridge only to be pushed back several times. A reporter for *Time* magazine described the vicious battle:

> Hell burst around the leathernecks as they moved up the barren face of the ridge. Everywhere along the assault line, men dropped. To continue looked impossible. But, all glory forever to the bravest men I ever saw, the line did not break. The casualties were unthinkable, but the assault force never turned back.[49]

By the end of the day the fighting had quieted down, but the marines expected further assaults by the NKPA. At 2:30 the next morning the enemy struck again. Successive waves of North Korean troops attacked the marine positions, but with the help of air cover and artillery the marines fought back the assault. Soon they were advancing on the North Koreans who, pounded by Corsair aircraft and U.S. artillery, began to fall back. By the evening of August 18 the marines had taken Obong-ni Ridge and its North Korean defenders were retreating beyond the Naktong. Meeting up with the men of the Thirty-fourth Division the following day, the marines took prisoners of what remained of the NKPA Fourth Division, the rest having escaped back across the river.

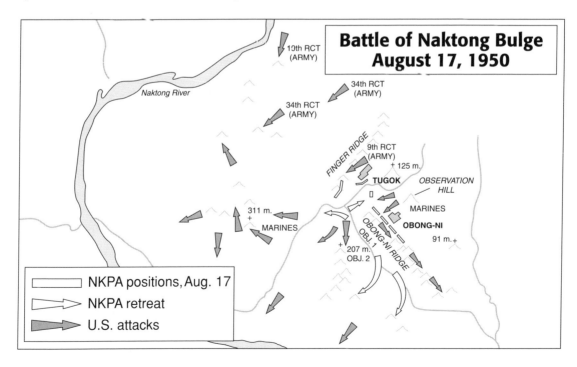

On the Perimeter

First Lieutenant Bill Glasgow was one of the defenders of the Pusan Perimeter. He recalls some of his experiences on the line in *No Bugles, No Drums: An Oral History of the Korean War* by Rudy Tomedi:

> I arrived in Korea with the 2nd Infantry Division from Fort Lewis, Washington, around the middle of August, and as soon as we got there they busted us down into battalions so they could spread us around and put us where we could do the most good.
>
> My first real hard fight was on the thirty-first of August, in front of the Naktong River. I was a first lieutenant and I had an infantry platoon, about forty men, and with those forty men I was supposed to hold twenty-six hundred yards of front.
>
> So what I did was occupy these four little hilltops. There was no other way to do it. You can't stretch forty men along almost a mile and a half of front. The only chance I had of holding that sector was to hold onto the high ground.
>
> That night the better part of two North Korean regiments walked through my position. We knew they were coming. We could see the Naktong River from our foxholes, and the rafts that were hidden just under the water on the other side of the river. And toward dusk we could see all these little pointed heads moving around in the rice paddies. So we knew we were going to be hit that night.
>
> They came through about midnight, but before they came across we saw a strange torchlight procession in the hills across the river. I tried to get my artillery forward observer to fire on it, but he wouldn't call in the fire mission because he thought the North Koreans had lined up a bunch of refugees and were making them march around by torchlight. . . .
>
> At about nine o'clock we lost all communications. Probably the North Koreans had already infiltrated and cut the telephone wires. Around eleven o'clock the order went out to withdraw, but of course my platoon never got it. We were still there at midnight when the two regiments of North Koreans came across the river.

The victory at the Naktong Bulge saved the vital supply line from Pusan to Taegu and dealt the NKPA a blow with the destruction of its Fourth Division. But fighting would continue along the Pusan Perimeter until the middle of September, when the Eighth Army was finally able to break out of its stronghold.

Breakout

On September 15, 1950, UN forces made an amphibious landing at Inchon, far behind the North Korean lines. The plan was conceived by General Douglas MacArthur with the goal of cutting off the NKPA's long supply line from North Korea and recapturing the South Korean capital of Seoul. It was also designed to trap the North Korean army between two UN forces in a hammer-and-anvil maneuver. MacArthur envisioned the Eighth Army as the hammer that would smash the NKPA against the anvil, the X Corps of the Inchon invasion. But first the

Eighth would have to break free from the Pusan Perimeter.

The breakout began on September 16. It was expected that when the North Korean troops around the perimeter learned of the amphibious assault far to their rear they would break ranks and run for safety. But the news never reached them, and so the NKPA fought as tenaciously as it had for the past six weeks. American air support began the next day, with aircraft dropping bombs and napalm on the NKPA troops. Slowly the combination of ground and air assaults took its toll on the North Koreans, who began fleeing north in disarray as the Eighth Army pushed forward. As UN aircraft controlled the skies and troops and armor rumbled along the main roads, the North Koreans took to the hills, melting away into the Korean countryside. The NKPA was no longer a credible fighting force.

Elements of the Eighth Army and the X Corps finally joined up on September 26 near the town of Osan. It was a symbolic linkage, for it occurred not far from the place where Task Force Smith, the first U.S. troops to fight in the Korean War, was destroyed by the North Korean army. This time the United States was victorious, and it seemed that the war might soon come to an end. But there was still a surprise in store for MacArthur's forces in Korea—and it would come swiftly and silently from beyond Korea's northern border.

Chapter 5

Unsan: China Enters the War

On the morning of October 15, 1950, an airplane carrying President Harry S. Truman touched down on Wake Island, a small, triangular atoll in the Pacific Ocean. Awaiting the president was General Douglas MacArthur, commander in chief of the United Nations (UN) forces in Korea. Among the many issues the two men discussed that morning, one of the most important to Truman was limiting the war in Korea. He asked MacArthur about the possibility that Communist China would enter the war on the North Korean side. The general replied that the chances of that happening were "very little. Had they interfered in the first or second months it would have been decisive. . . . Now that we have bases for our Air Force in Korea, if the Chinese tried to get down to Pyongyang, there would be the greatest slaughter."[50]

The Wake Island conference lasted less than two hours. It ended on an upbeat note with Truman pinning a Distinguished Service Medal on the general's uniform. Then the two men boarded their separate planes, Truman heading back to Washington and MacArthur to his headquarters in Tokyo. As their aircraft left Wake Island behind, neither knew that Chinese Communist troops were already crossing into North Korea.

China Prepares for War

The Chinese province of Manchuria lies just north of North Korea, with the Yalu River separating the two Communist countries. With the decisive triumphs of the North Korean People's Army (NKPA) over U.S. and South Korean armies in the early days of the war, China had little to fear from the UN forces. But as the North Koreans were driven north after the Inchon invasion and the breakout from the Pusan Perimeter, concern in China rose. If UN troops managed to advance all the way to the Yalu, what would stop them from crossing the river and invading Manchuria?

U.S. soldiers and South Korean guerrillas celebrate as they cross the 38th parallel in October 1950.

Marshal Peng Dehuai, field commander of the army in western China, recalled these fears in his memoirs: "The U.S. occupation of Korea, separated from China only by a river, would threaten northeast China. . . . The United States could find a pretext at any time to launch a war of aggression against China. The tiger wanted to eat human beings; when it would do so would depend on its appetite." With fear of the American "tiger" growing in China, Peng suggested that "we should dispatch troops to Korea to safeguard our national construction."[51]

Had anyone in the United States been listening, perhaps the possibility of a Chinese invasion would have been taken more seriously. But U.S. plans to enter North Korea had already been set in motion. On September 27 Truman had approved MacArthur's new orders to "conduct military operations north of the 38th parallel," with the objective of "the destruction of the North Korean Armed Forces."[52] On October 1 two important events occurred: MacArthur called for the surrender of all North Korean forces, and troops of the Republic of Korea (ROK)—South Korea—

began crossing the 38th parallel. A week later, U.S. troops would do the same.

Chinese premier Chou En-lai announced on October 2 that the Chinese people "will not tolerate foreign aggres- sion and will not stand aside should the imperialists wantonly invade the territory of their neighbor."[53] MacArthur consid- ered this warning merely a bluff. Besides, with UN forces already moving against

The Drive to the Yalu

SOVIET UNION

CHINA

Manchuria

Yalu River

October 26, 1950

Pyongyang

NORTH KOREA

June 25, 1950

UN forces cross 38th parallel October 1, 1950

38TH PARALLEL

Seoul

SOUTH KOREA

UN drives
NKPA retreat lines

the NKPA, MacArthur predicted a quick end to the war and the return of U.S. troops home by Christmas. Plans were being made to redeploy some U.S. troops out of Korea. Some additional troop shipments and deliveries of ammunition to Korea were canceled. The *New York Times* boasted that, "except for unexpected developments along the frontiers of the peninsula, we can now be easy in our minds as to the military outcome."[54]

The United States was totally unprepared for the "unexpected development" that was about to take place.

UN Forces Push North

The first half of October 1950 saw UN forces pushing north past the 38th parallel and making their way through North Korea. The ROK Third and Capital Divisions were advancing along the east coast of Korea. They captured the port of Wonsan on October 10. MacArthur's plan to take North Korea involved splitting the U.S. forces, a controversial strategy. He sent the Eighth Army up the western side of the peninsula toward the North Korean capital of Pyongyang. The X Corps was to be ferried by sea to Wonsan on the east coast, and from there it would head west to link up with the Eighth. On October 19 Pyongyang fell to troops of the First Cavalry Division, and ROK units were steadily advancing toward the Yalu against diminishing NKPA resistance.

On October 25 elements of the ROK First and Sixth Divisions headed out from

a town named Kunu as they continued their drive toward the Yalu. About a mile and a half past Unsan, a town about halfway between the 38th parallel and the Yalu in North Korea, the Fifteenth Regiment of the First Division encountered mortar fire near a bridge. The ROK troops engaged the enemy, which fought back tenaciously. The ROKs took a prisoner but were puzzled because, although he wore a NKPA uniform, he did not speak either Korean or Japanese. In fact, their prisoner was Chinese, and in his native language he told of some twenty thousand Chinese troops hiding in the hills north and east of Unsan. This disturbing news was passed along to intelligence officers at Eighth Army headquarters, and soon other Chinese prisoners were providing corroborative information about the presence of a large Chinese force in North Korea. But even with this intelligence, U.S. military planners had no idea of the true number of Chinese soldiers in North Korea.

Throughout the late summer of 1950 there had been a gradual migration of Chinese army units from the southern and central regions of China into Manchuria in the northwest. When the Korean War started, U.S. intelligence estimated the strength of the Communist army in Manchuria at about 115,000 soldiers. By late October, however, further estimates put the number of troops at approximately 316,000, with an additional 147,000 possibly there but unconfirmed. In all, this in-

Operation Yo-Yo

Operation Chromite, the invasion of Inchon, had been a stunning success. The NKPA was on the run, and General Douglas MacArthur was ready to conquer the entire Korean peninsula and end the war. But rather than continue the advance begun at Inchon, MacArthur decided to stage another amphibious operation, this time at the port of Wonsan on Korea's east coast. The plan called for the First Marine Division, the amphibious element of X Corps, to travel from Inchon by ship south around the lower end of Korea and up the east coast of the peninsula to Wonsan. From there the marines would chase the North Koreans toward the Yalu River, the border between North Korea and China.

The marines loaded onto ships at Inchon harbor on October 9 and 10, 1950, and the assault force sailed on October 16. The target date for the landing at Wonsan was October 20, but soon an unforeseen problem arose: The Wonsan harbor was laced with mines ready to blow any ships that approached out of the water. The October 21 landing day was postponed, and

twenty-one minesweeping ships were dispatched to Wonsan to remove the mines. While the minesweepers were doing their job, the ships carrying the First Marines could do nothing but wait. So they slowly sailed first one way and then the other outside of the harbor, to the distinct displeasure of the marines on board. For a group of fighting men ready to make an assault, the waiting was intolerable, and they began derisively calling their back-and-forth journey "Operation Yo-Yo."

Conditions on the cramped ships were less than ideal, as food shortages threatened and the environment was ripe for a breakout of disease. On October 26 the mines were finally cleared and the marines, after sixteen days of being crowded onto the ships, began to disembark at Wonsan. But it was less an assault than a stroll onto the docks. For the ROK army had secured the port from enemy fire six days before the marines landed. Operation Yo-Yo had deprived the First Marine Division of the chance to make another dramatic landing as they had at Inchon.

dicated a Chinese force more than 450,000 strong poised to enter the war—a formidable force if it were deployed.

Chinese "Volunteers"

By late October a total of about 180,000 Chinese troops had slipped quietly across the Yalu River into North Korea. Reinforcements crossing the river in November would bring the total of Chinese forces in North Korea to around 300,000. Although the majority of these troops were veterans of the regular Chinese army, they were referred to as the Chinese People's Volunteers. This title created the

pretext that China was not officially confronting the United States in the war. "By labeling these troops as volunteer outfits," reported a U.S. intelligence officer, "China can claim to the world that no formal intervention has occurred."[55] To the UN Command in Korea, the Chinese troops were known as the Chinese Communist Forces (CCF).

The CCF moved at night because under the cover of darkness they could avoid detection by UN aircraft that flew unopposed over the Korean skies. Military historian Roy Appleman describes a typical CCF march:

The day's march began after dark at 1900 [7:00 P.M.] and ended at 0300 [3:00 A.M.] the next morning. Defense measures against aircraft were to be completed before 0530 [5:30 A.M.]. Every man, animal, and piece of equipment were to be concealed and camouflaged. During daylight only bivouac scouting parties moved ahead to select the next day's bivouac area. When CCF units were compelled for any reason to march by day, they were under standing orders for every man to stop in his tracks and remain motionless if aircraft appeared overhead. Officers were empowered to shoot down immediately any man who violated this order.[56]

CCF troops were experts at waging war with a minimum of supplies and amenities. They were able to cover great distances rapidly at night on foot; one division traveled eighteen miles a day over Korea's mountainous terrain for eighteen straight days. In addition, they were experts in the art of camouflage and could subsist on meager portions of rice as their daily rations. The CCF had few tanks, little artillery, and no air force. But what they lacked in modern weaponry they made up in guerrilla warfare expertise. Their tactics for battle had been laid out by Mao Zedong, chairman of the Chinese Communist Party: "Enemy advancing, we retreat; enemy entrenched, we harass; enemy exhausted, we attack; enemy retreating, we pursue."[57] As the ROK army was finding out, the Chinese "volunteers" were formidable foes.

Fighting the Chinese

The ROK First Division's Fifteenth Regiment continued its battle with the Chinese troops throughout the day of October 25. The ROK troops were surprised at the ferocity with which their enemy fought. The Fifteenth's advance toward the Yalu had been stopped cold. Other ROK troops also encountered stiff CCF resistance: The Twelfth Regiment was hit just outside of Unsan, and the Second Regiment was trapped between two Chinese roadblocks, resulting in some 350 ROK casualties. By the afternoon of October 26 the ROK forces were retreating, and it appeared that the CCF would soon have the town of Unsan surrounded.

Although the ROK troops estimated that they were facing at least a division of Chinese troops, or about nine thousand men, the U.S. leaders were less than concerned about this new enemy. An intelligence report on October 26 said only that there appeared to be "some further reinforcement of North Korean units with personnel taken from the Chinese Communist Forces, in order to assist in the defense of the border approaches," and that there were "no indications of open intervention on the part of Chinese Communist Forces in Korea."[58] Over the next several days, the situation improved somewhat for the ROKs at Unsan. UN aircraft dropped much needed supplies and ammunition to the ROK forces, who were actually making some limited gains against the CCF. Several additional captured Chinese soldiers confirmed the accounts of earlier prisoners about the number of CCF troops in North Korea.

By now, General Walton Walker, commander of the Eighth Army, was beginning to reconsider the extent of CCF involvement. At first he discounted the stories of the Chinese prisoners as just so much propaganda. But as more information about the losses being inflicted on the ROK forces in and around Unsan came in, Walker's concern increased. On October 28 he ordered the First Cavalry Division to end its security duties in Pyongyang, move north through Unsan, and head for the Yalu River. The next day the division's Eighth Cavalry Regiment left Pyongyang, followed shortly by the Fifth Regiment.

As the First Cavalry made its way north, CCF troops once more engaged the ROKs, ambushing their positions and

U.S. Marines advance toward Chinese Communist Forces (CCF) positions near Unsan. The CCF proved to be a formidable enemy.

sending much of the South Korean force fleeing into the hills. Soon the Americans would also be battling a determined Chinese enemy.

Whistles and Bugles

By November 1, 1950, elements of the Eighth Cavalry were positioned around Unsan to counter Chinese attacks on the remaining ROK units. The First Battalion was deployed in an arc about a mile north of Unsan; its right flank was protected by the Samtan River, but its left flank was vulnerable. There was a mile-wide gap between this end of the First Battalion's line and the Second Battalion, which had taken up a position west of Unsan. The Third Battalion was dug in along the Nammyon River southwest of Unsan, about three miles above a Chinese roadblock.

Meanwhile, the CCF were on the move. An U.S. aerial spotter radioed an ominous report to an artillery battalion: "This is the strangest sight I have ever seen. There are two large columns of enemy infantry moving southeast. . . . Our shells are landing right in their columns and they keep coming."[59] After attacking the ROK Fifteenth Regiment all that afternoon, by 5:00 P.M. the CCF began to engage the Eighth Cavalry Regiment. Another mass Chinese assault at 7:30 pushed the First Battalion's right flank back some four hundred yards. Before long the CCF advanced to the gap between the First and Second Battalions

and began moving through it to the rear of the Second Battalion.

The eerie sounds of whistles and bugles heralded the Chinese attack on the Second Battalion. Such primitive signaling devices were necessary because the smaller units of the CCF had no radios or telephones for communication. The Second soon found itself encircled by the Chinese forces. Unlike previous assaults, at Unsan the CCF employed a new weapon against UN forces: Soviet-made rockets fired from launchers mounted on trucks. Although not very accurate, the rockets did manage to blow up an ammunition truck before being forced to move out of range of UN artillery fire. By late in the day it was obvious that the situation for the UN forces around Unsan was desperate. They just were no match for the CCF, which now had them virtually surrounded.

Withdrawal

By 11:00 P.M. on November 1, word came down for Eighth Cavalry Regiment and the remnants of the ROK Fifteenth Regiment to retreat. The plan was for the First and Second Battalions to withdraw through Unsan, down a road that led southeast from the town, then across the Kuryong River and south to safety. The Third Battalion would bring up the rear. Getting past Unsan proved to be a problem, as heavy gunfire indicated that the town was already held by the Chinese. Most of the First and Second Battalions, with their

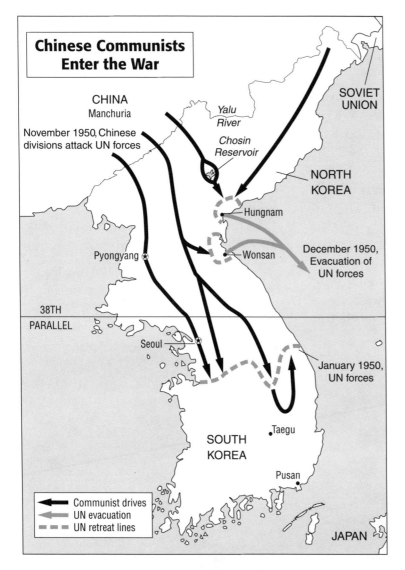

Chinese Communists Enter the War

CHINA
Manchuria

November 1950, Chinese divisions attack UN forces

Yalu River

Chosin Reservoir

SOVIET UNION

NORTH KOREA

Hungnam

Pyongyang

Wonsan

December 1950, Evacuation of UN forces

38TH PARALLEL

Seoul

January 1950, UN forces

Taegu

SOUTH KOREA

Pusan

JAPAN

→ Communist drives
→ UN evacuation
--- UN retreat lines

CCF troops blocking the road. Coming under sudden attack, a truck pulling a howitzer swerved into a ditch, leaving the overturned howitzer blocking the road. All attempts to clear the road under enemy fire failed, leaving the main escape route from Unsan blocked. In the confusion, the men at the road junction took to the hills to effect their withdrawal. Throughout the night and into the next morning, stragglers from the First and Second Battalions wandered into the town of Ipsok. The First had suffered more than 250 casualties and had lost about half its mortars and heavy weapons.

That left the Third Battalion still trapped, surrounded by the CCF south of Unsan. Because the battalion had not yet come under fire from the enemy, the men of the Third assumed that their withdrawal would go smoothly. Major Robert Ormond, commanding officer of the Third Battalion, knew that the main road south was blocked. Ormond devised a cross-country escape route and then sent an officer to find a suitable place to cross

trucks, artillery pieces, and tanks, managed to escape through or along the east side of Unsan and then headed south toward a fork in the road about a mile south of Unsan.

Just beyond the fork in the road, the retreating column was fired on by groups of the Nammyon River. In the meantime, the Third Battalion loaded up its vehicles and waited for the signal to move out.

Rescue

At about 3:00 A.M. on November 2, a column of what was assumed to be ROK troops was allowed to pass into the Third Battalion area and march up to the battalion command post. Suddenly a bugle sounded and gunfire erupted. The column was actually a company of CCF troops, and their bold assault had taken the battalion completely by surprise. At the same time, other Chinese soldiers attacked from across the Nammyon River. In vicious hand-to-hand combat, the Chi-

nese soldiers attacked with small arms, grenades, and explosives called satchel charges. Many of the U.S. soldiers were jolted out of their sleep by the attack. "I thought I was dreaming," recalled one lieutenant, "when I heard a bugle sounding taps and the beat of horses' hooves in the distance. Then, as though they came out of a burst of smoke, shadowy figures started shooting and bayoneting everybody they could find."[60]

The hand-to-hand combat lasted for about a half hour before the Chinese

U.S. Marines cover the advance of UN soldiers at Unsan. The fighting at Unsan was the first encounter between UN and CCF troops in the Korean War.

Retrieving the Wounded

Even though the rescue mission for the Third Battalion was called off, there were still many wounded soldiers who had to be brought back to aid stations behind the lines. Surprisingly, the Communists actually helped the UN forces retrieve their wounded, as recalled by Captain Norman Allen in Donald Knox's *The Korean War: Pusan to Chosin: An Oral History:*

> It was during this withdrawal that we first experienced that business with the wounded. Walking wounded captured by the Chinese were allowed to return to our lines. They told us the Communists would allow us to pick up our other wounded, that they would be placed along the road, and vehicles coming for them would not be fired on. One medic said, "Give me a jeep. I'll go." He was joined by other guys. I placed two tanks across the road and told them to cover the jeep. If anyone fired on it, they were to plaster the areas on either side of the road. A few minutes later the jeep returned carrying four or five wounded. The poor souls were dropped off. The jeep spun around and again raced down the road. This time it was followed by several others. The wounded told of being carried by the Chinese to the road on stretchers marked "Donated by the American Red Cross." The jeeps rushed back and forth until it became quite dark. Then we fell back and went into a regimental perimeter.

pulled back. Sporadic fighting continued until daylight when UN aircraft struck at the enemy troops, keeping them huddling under cover for the rest of the day. During that time, some 170 wounded were brought inside the Third Battalion perimeter. In the afternoon, a plane flew over and dropped an encouraging message: A rescue force was on the way. The task of rescuing the Third Battalion fell to the Fifth Cavalry Regiment, which was assembled about eight miles south of where the Third was trapped. As soon as two enemy-held ridges were secured by other elements of the Fifth Regiment, the rescue team would rush in with trucks and tanks and bring the Third Battalion out.

As the afternoon wore on, the Fifth Cavalry waited for the command to begin the mission. But the order never came; the ridges could not be secured. "Near to 4:00 P.M.," remembered Captain Norman Allen, leader of the rescue force, "I had the tanks and trucks again turn over their engines. Colonel Treacy came up and told me the 1st Battalion had not been able to seize the first ridge, even after the 2d Battalion had been thrown in to help out. The mission was canceled."[61] Soon another plane flew over the Third Battalion's perimeter with another message: Rescue was not coming, and the battalion should withdraw as best it could on its own.

The Lost Battalion

The decimated Third Battalion bravely held on against continued CCF assaults for the next two days. By November 4 there were some 250 wounded in the Third Battalion perimeter and only about 200 able-bodied men. After a brief discussion of their situation, the men decided that those who were still unharmed should try to escape from the perimeter. After scouting out an escape route, the men began their retreat at about 2:30 P.M., leaving the wounded with Captain Clarence Anderson, the battalion surgeon, to be captured by the Chinese.

As the men reached the east side of the perimeter, the Chinese began a barrage of white phosphorous shells, creating a smoke screen to cover a new attack. After traveling east and then southwest all night, the escaping group approached Ipsok. The next day, however, they found themselves surrounded by Chinese troops, forcing them to break into small groups to increase their chances of survival. It was a last desperate plan that had no chance of working. Most of the men were either killed or captured that day.

In all, the Eighth Cavalry Division suffered about six hundred casualties in the action at Unsan. It was the first encounter between U.S. and Chinese troops in the Korean War, but it would not be the last. The U.S. Marines would confront the Chinese at a forbidding frozen lake in northeastern North Korea.

Chapter 6

Escape from the Chosin Reservoir

By late November 1950, the leaders of the United Nations (UN) military operation in Korea faced a difficulty that would have a major impact on their conduct in the next phase of the war. The problem was simply trying to figure out what the Chinese were up to. The one thing General Douglas MacArthur and his field commanders knew for sure was that the Chinese Communist Forces (CCF) had indeed entered the war. But beyond that fact, everything else was speculation. How many Chinese soldiers were in North Korea? How many more awaited mobilization in Manchuria? How experienced were the CCF troops, and what kind of weapons did they have? And, perhaps the most puzzling question of all, what had happened to the Chinese troops that had virtually annihilated the Eighth Cavalry Division in the west? Rather than continuing their advance through the UN lines, the Chinese forces had simply disappeared into the mountains of North Korea.

Unfortunately, as the Korean winter tightened its grip on the UN forces, no one had the answers to these questions. In fact, by Thanksgiving of 1950, it appeared that the war might even be drawing to a close.

Home by Christmas

U.S. intelligence estimates placed the number of Chinese troops in Korea at anywhere from thirty thousand to one hundred thousand (actually, there were about three times the latter figure by the end of November). Despite the varying numbers being reported, however, the evidence indicated that a large force of CCF soldiers had crossed into North Korea, posing a considerable threat. MacArthur seemed to change his opinion on this evidence daily, at first declaring that the Chinese had "only limited objectives in mind," only later to assert that the CCF was "a serious proximate threat." The general weighed his options, which ultimately

Two U.S. soldiers enjoy a Thanksgiving Day feast in 1950. General MacArthur was convinced that U.S. troops would be back home by Christmas of that year.

came down to three: "I could go forward, remain immobile, or withdraw."[62] Finally, convincing himself that the Chinese would not mount a major offensive in North Korea, MacArthur decided to go forward, completing the drive to the Yalu River to rout the North Koreans and win the war.

Thursday, November 23, 1950, was Thanksgiving Day, and the troops in Korea enjoyed a special treat: a traditional holiday feast of turkey, dressing, sweet potatoes, and cranberry sauce brought up to the front lines. The front had been quiet for some time, and the troops hoped that the advance to the Yalu would be swift and low on casualties. MacArthur, too, was confident in his decision to push on. The next day, the day the advance was to begin, he remarked, "If this operation is successful, I hope I can get the boys home by Christmas."[63] Soon U.S. newspapers were heralding the "Home by Christmas Offensive" that would assure victory and have the troops home for the holidays. But MacArthur, the acclaimed mastermind of the daring Inchon invasion, had made a strategic blunder that would prolong the war far beyond Christmas 1950.

In a move that seemed to defy military logic, MacArthur had separated his two forces, the Eighth Army and the X Corps, after the successful landing at Inchon. The Eighth Army was pushing toward the Yalu in the west, while the X Corps, which had been taken around the Korean peninsula to the port of Wonsan, was advancing in the east. After the initial appearance and then disappearance of the CCF at Unsan, resistance lightened considerably as the UN forces pushed the battle-weary North Korean People's Army (NKPA) troops back toward the Yalu. But the CCF was about to come out of hiding, with deadly results.

The Chosin Reservoir

On November 24, 1950, MacArthur's "Home by Christmas" campaign began as the Eighth Army initiated its assault in the northwest and X Corps moved out in

Marines of the X Corps land at Wonsan during a surprise amphibious invasion. MacArthur's decision to separate the X Corps from the Eighth Army had disastrous consequences.

the northeast. The two forces were to eventually link up and proceed north to the Yalu. The main combat element of the X Corps was the First Marine Division, commanded by Major General Oliver P. Smith. This division consisted of three infantry regiments, the First, Fifth, and Seventh Marines, and the Eleventh Marines, an artillery regiment. X Corps also included elements of the U.S. Army's Seventh Infantry Division. After landing at Wonsan on October 26, the marines had headed up a winding road that would be designated the Main Supply Route (MSR) through a village called Koto to the town of Hagaru. Already nearly abandoned when the marines arrived, Hagaru stood on a four-thousand-foot plateau at the southern tip of a large artificial lake known as the Chosin Reservoir.

The Chosin (also called Changjin) Reservoir had been built by the Japanese during their occupation of Korea, which began in 1910. For the push north, General Smith chose Hagaru as the marines' base of operations because of its location at the foot of the reservoir. Two roads led north from the town, one on the east side of the reservoir toward Sinhung and a northwestern road that meandered through the rugged terrain toward the town of Yudam. Smith, who was not at all convinced that MacArthur's assessment of the Chinese threat was correct, began to prepare his force for a tough campaign. Engineers immediately went to work at Hagaru, widening the road so that tanks and heavy bulldozers could get into the town. His forces also began construction of a 3,200-foot airstrip. For the support of his army, Smith had a field hospital constructed, as well as supply depots for ammunition, food, fuel, and other necessities. Colonel Alpha Bowser, Smith's chief of operations, recalled that "all these preparations, and many others—all the result of General Smith's foresight—were ultimately to save the lives of thousands of fighting men and may well have saved the Marine division as a whole."[64]

Engaging the Enemy

On November 25, the Fifth and Seventh Regiments of the First Marine Division began advancing along the road northwest of the Chosin Reservoir, moving through the narrow Toktong Pass, which is located about eight miles west of Hagaru. Their destination was Yudam, from which they hoped to begin the final offensive of the war. The plan was to advance west and link up with the Eighth Army, and, from there, the combined forces would push north and destroy the NKPA. The rest of the First Division took up positions along the MSR south of Hagaru to make sure that the road stayed open. The next day three battalions of the army's Seventh Infantry Division moved up the road along the eastern side of the reservoir, heading for a position some thirteen miles north of Hagaru. Air cover for the operation would be provided by the First Marine Aircraft Wing.

By the morning of November 27, the marine and army forces were in place, and the X Corps offensive began. The marines at Yudam moved west but soon were engaged in a fierce fight with CCF troops. "We were pushing ahead of everybody," remarked Captain Elmer Dodson of the marines, "when we ran smack into what seemed like most of the Chinese from China."[65] In fact, some sixty thousand CCF troops, eight Chinese divisions, were waiting for the First Marine Division in the hills surrounding the Chosin Reservoir, and they were determined to destroy the marines. The fighting continued

U.S. troops near the Chosin Reservoir ready their artillery. Defeat at Chosin made MacArthur realize that the war would last considerably longer than anticipated.

throughout the day, but the marines could make no headway against the CCF troops. That night the Chinese mounted a major assault against Yudam in temperatures that hovered around twenty below zero. They also attacked Fox Company, a group of 240 marines guarding the Toktong Pass on the road to Hagaru, in a battle that would last for five days.

The three battalions of the army's Seventh Division east of the reservoir fared no better. The Chinese attacked their positions and eventually surrounded them. But the X Corps commander, General Edward Almond, still did not grasp the extent of the Chinese enemy his troops were facing. On a visit to the front Almond declared, "The enemy who is delaying you for the moment is nothing more than the remnants of Chinese divisions fleeing north. We're still attacking and we're going all the way to the Yalu. Don't let a bunch of Chinese laundrymen stop you."[66]

On the morning of November 28, the marines at Yudam began a counterattack against the CCF, but before long it became clear that they were suffering too many casualties for too little progress. They established a defensive perimeter around Yudam and fought off repeated

Frozen Chosin

Korea is a land of extreme temperatures, with scorching, humid summers and bitingly cold winters. At elevated locations such as the Chosin Reservoir plateau, the thermometer could reach twenty to thirty degrees below zero in the winter; howling winds made the climate even more dangerous. As quoted in *Breakout: The Chosin Reservoir Campaign, Korea 1950* by Martin Russ, General Oliver P. Smith did his best to outfit his men with proper winter clothing:

> I ordered the cold-weather gear to be issued from the beach dumps at [the port city of] Hungnam. . . . We outfitted the 7th Marines first because they were already in the high elevations. The gear consisted of mountain sleeping bags, alpaca-lined parkas, windproof trousers, heavy woolen socks, and shoe-pacs. The parkas were long Navy types, more suitable for standing watch aboard ship than long marches in the mountains. As to the shoe-pacs, they were really duck-hunter's boots—an invitation to frostbite in sub-zero temperatures.

Frostbite turned out to be an enemy every bit as dangerous as the Chinese. A navy battalion surgeon noted that "the effect on the line Marines was drastic. There were numerous cases of what appeared to be shock—but it was the shock of a terrific cold spell they weren't ready for." As Lieutenant Colonel Raymond Davis, a battalion commander with the Seventh Marines, recalled, "It was bad. My staff and I moved around among the troops, looking for the characteristic candle-white splotches that signaled frostbite; when we spotted it coming on, we would hustle the man to the nearest fire." Bare hands froze, and wet shoes and socks became stuck to the marines' feet. Inserts in the shoe-pacs that were supposed to be removed and dried every night remained sodden, causing constant foot problems. Of all the forces in Korea, the marines at the Chosin Reservoir suffered the worst because of the weather.

The intense cold played havoc with guns and equipment as well. Automatic weapons would fire only a single round at a time or sometimes none at all. Oil in tanks and trucks froze, making it impossible to start the vehicles. Even eating a meal became a struggle with the cold. Rations froze in their containers, and canteens burst because the water inside had turned to ice. Plasma could not be given to the wounded because it froze in its bottles.

But the X Corps at the Chosin Reservoir had a job to do—and they did it in the midst of the treacherous Korean winter.

U.S. Marines wait on an icy trail during the retreat from the Chosin Reservoir. A strong CCF army and freezing weather halted the UN drive to the Yalu.

attacks from the CCF. All around the Chosin Reservoir and along the MSR south from Hagaru, Chinese troops were besieging the marines and soldiers. At his headquarters in Tokyo, MacArthur met with the commanders of the Eighth Army and X Corps. Finally admitting that the UN Command was facing "an entirely new war,"[67] MacArthur gave the order to halt the drive to the Yalu and pull back the troops.

So the war would not be over nor the troops home by Christmas after all. And the fighting retreat that lay ahead for the First Marine Division would become one of the most famous episodes in the annals of the U.S. Marine Corps.

Attacking in a Different Direction

On November 30, 1950, Almond ordered Smith to bring the marine and army regiments back from the reservoir and assemble them at Hagaru in preparation to withdraw south down the MSR toward the town of Hamhung and its nearby port, Hungnam. Almond authorized Smith to

Life in Hagaru

Fred Lawson was a rifleman with the Third Battalion, Seventh Marines at the Battle of the Chosin Reservoir. After fierce fighting against the Chinese in Yudam, Lawson's company was ordered to withdraw to Hagaru at the southern end of the reservoir. After being harassed by sporadic Chinese fire all along the road, Lawson and his unit finally arrived in Hagaru. His description of the village is found in *No Bugles, No Drums: An Oral History of the Korean War* by Rudy Tomedi:

> Hagaru was a mess. It looked like a staging area. Tents were up, vehicles were parked side by side and bumper to bumper, supplies were piled up wherever there was an open space. Everything was crowded in close together, because the perimeter was so small. There was a little airstrip there, and planes were taking out the wounded and bringing in replacements. They were C-47s I believe, and I remember how big and slow and fat they looked coming into that field. The Chinese were in the hills all around Hagaru, and they shot at every plane coming in and going out.
>
> When we got there we didn't get a chance to rest, because we had to help hold the perimeter. We came in off the line in shifts, ate, and went right back out again.
>
> The Chinese kept hammering at the perimeter. They were all around us, and I'd already made up my mind that it was going to be a miracle if we got out of there. We'd had such an awful time just getting down to Hagaru from the reservoir, and that was only fifteen miles. We had another sixty to go [to get to the port of Hungnam], and I just couldn't see any way we were going to make it.

destroy as much equipment as necessary in order to facilitate the speedy retreat of his troops. Smith, a marine who had little regard for his army superior, coldly replied that "my command is perfectly able to bring its equipment out intact."[68]

The marines' withdrawal from Yudam to Hagaru began on the morning of December 1. It was to be a dangerous trek, as Lieutenant Colonel Raymond Murray recalled: "Hagaru was fourteen miles down the road, but there were a hell of a lot of Chinese between us and them."[69] With a single tank in the lead, the column moved out. Attacking CCF troops all along the way, the marines brought their dead and seriously wounded down the road in jeeps and trucks, while artillery pieces brought up the rear. Because the column would have to go through the Toktong Pass, where Fox Company had been fighting off the Chinese for five days, a rescue force was assembled. Hoping to catch the Chinese by surprise, the rescue party left the main column on the road and headed out over the rough terrain of the Korean countryside. According to Lieutenant Colonel Raymond Davis, leader of the rescue party, its mission was as simple as it was important: "Some fellow Marines were in trouble. We were going to rescue them and nothing was going to stand in our way. . . . By seizing the [Toktong] pass we would unlock the gate and hold it open for the rest of the Marines in Yudam-ni."[70] Davis's rescue party reached Fox Company on December 1. Fox had suffered 118 casualties out of a force of 240, but it had held out against thousands of enemy troops.

The last of the marines reached Hagaru on December 4. The First Division had suffered more than twenty-three hundred casualties, many of them due to the frigid weather. Reinforcements were brought for the next phase of the withdrawal: the fight

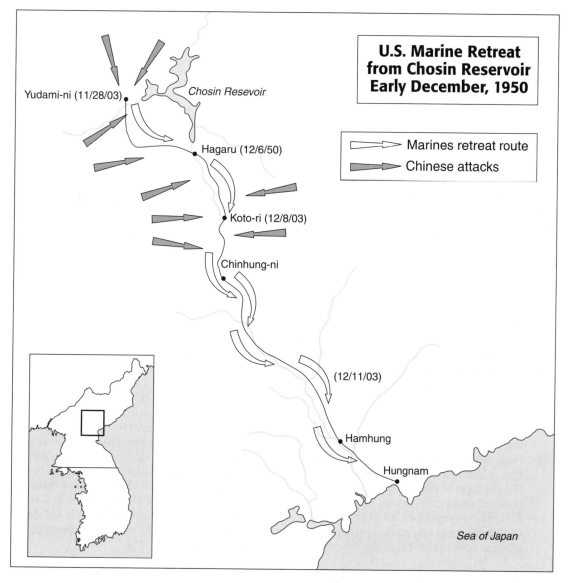

U.S. Marine Retreat
from Chosin Reservoir
Early December, 1950

down the MSR toward Koto and then on to Hamhung. For several days reporters had been arriving at Hagaru, preparing to cover the marines' withdrawal. One reporter asked General Smith if the marines were, in fact, retreating. "Certainly not," Smith replied. "There can be no retreat when there is no rear. You can't retreat, or even withdraw, when you're surrounded. The only thing you can do is break out, and in order to do that you have to attack, and that's what we're about to do."[71] By the time Smith's comment hit U.S. newspapers, it had been transformed into a more dramatic, if inaccurate, quote: "Retreat, hell! We're not retreating; we're just attacking in a different direction."[72] The phrase ultimately became a part of Marine Corps lore.

Breaking Out

At 6:30 A.M. on December 6, a column of one thousand vehicles and fourteen thousand troops headed south down the MSR from Hagaru. The survivors of the army battalions east of the Chosin Reservoir also joined the column. The Seventh Marines led the withdrawal. The Fifth

Flying into Hagaru

The survival of the marines at Hagaru would have been in serious doubt had not it been for the airlifting of supplies by the venerable C-47 aircraft and their courageous pilots. The twin engine C-47, the military version of the civilian DC-3 passenger aircraft, was a rugged workhorse that saw action from World War II to Vietnam. And its pilots had to be just as rugged to muscle the plane in and out of the small airstrip at Hagaru. In his book *Korea: The First War We Lost*, Bevin Alexander describes the difficulties of flying a C-47 into Hagaru:

This fabulous aircraft not only was the workhorse of the military forces in Korea, but was required to perform under conditions and on fields that were ludicrously tiny—either carved out of broken ground like the strip at Hagaru, or laid out on the floors of minuscule valleys with towering mountains ranging on all sides. And the C-47 produced. Any passenger who flew often in Korea (and it was the only means

of rapid travel available) came to think of it as perfectly normal for a heavily laden C-47 to drop over a high mountain ridge, fall like a stone toward a postage-stamp field, brake almost the moment the craft hit the ground, and then come to a shuddering rest within a dozen or a score of yards of the end of the runway. Hairy as this experience was, it was as nothing compared to a takeoff: the pilot revved the engines until the craft fought to break away; then, when it seemed that plane would tear itself apart from the strain, the pilot released the brakes and the C-47 burst down the short runway, got quickly aloft, and, its engines straining for every ounce of power, climbed just above the rapidly rising ground and over the final ridgeline. Often the planes cleared the last ridge by a few feet. Of all the men in Korea who earned respect for their skill and daring, none were held in higher esteem than the pilots of the C-47s.

Marines acted as the rear guard, holding the Hagaru perimeter to fend off enemy attack. Around-the-clock air support from marine aircraft covered the advancing column and probed each side of the MSR for enemy troops. The first objective was to reach Koto, nine miles south of Hagaru.

From the outset it was a fighting withdrawal, with the Seventh Marines engaging CCF troops who had taken up positions on the ridges all along the road. The marines battled past Chinese roadblocks, ambushes, and demolished bridges. "Enemy units fought savagely," recalled a marine private, "mounting attacks from ridges towering above the road, setting ambushes and executing the wounded when hospital trucks could be isolated from the rest of the column."[73] The column finally entered Koto near midnight on December 7 after suffering another six hundred casualties. The next stage of the withdrawal would take the marines thirty-seven miles from Koto to Hamhung. But there was a major obstacle to overcome first.

Three and one-half miles south of Koto, the Chinese had blown a twenty-nine-foot hole in the road where a bridge had once spanned a deep chasm just north of an area called the Funchilin Pass. The road was the only way to get the column's tanks and trucks through to Hamhung, but it was impossible to go around the damage due to steep, rocky ridges on either side. "The enemy could not have picked a better spot to give us trouble," recalled General Smith. Fortunately, Smith's engineering officer,

Lieutenant Colonel John Partridge, had an idea. Partridge estimated that four sections of steel bridge spans known as Treadway bridges would cross the gap in the road. But these spans would have to be flown in from Japan and dropped by parachute— something that had never been done before. Some Treadways were accidentally dropped in enemy territory and one was damaged, but the airdrop was ultimately successful. U.S. Army engineers worked feverishly to cover the gap, and soon tanks and trucks were rolling over the Treadways. The vehicles were guided through the night by soldiers with flashlights. By December 10, the entire column had gone through the Funchilin Pass.

To the Sea

Chinese resistance diminished as the column moved south through the bitter winter. At the town of Chinhung, many of the troops boarded trucks or railroad cars to ride for the rest of the evacuation. From Chinhung, it was a relatively uneventful journey to Hamhung and then to Hungnam on Korea's east coast. Still, between Koto and Hamhung, the column suffered nearly 350 additional casualties. And Chinese and North Korean troops continued to advance toward the defensive perimeter around Hamhung-Hungnam. Waiting at the port were navy transport ships ready to evacuate the marines and soldiers of X Corps from North Korea. On December 11, troops began boarding the ships along with their equipment, supplies, and vehicles. In addition, countless Korean refugees fleeing the Communists clamored to find space on the vessels.

Over the next two weeks, the withdrawal by sea continued. On Christmas Eve 1950, the last troops left the beaches of Hungnam. In what was perhaps an appropriate finale to the withdrawal, engineers detonated stockpiles of ordnance that had to be left behind and set fire to supplies remaining at the port. As the last ships sailed south toward the safety of Pusan,

black smoke hung in a pall over the port that had been abandoned to the enemy.

Of the withdrawal from the Chosin Reservoir, *Time* magazine said, "It was defeat—the worst the United States ever suffered."[74] Many who were there held a different opinion. "Everyone who got out saw it as a victory, because we weren't sup-

UN soldiers board transport ships on the beach at Hungnam to be evacuated into South Korean territory.

posed to get out,"[75] recalled a navy corpsman. There were, however, many who did not make it out. The First Marine Division suffered more than 4,400 battle casualties, including 718 killed. More than 7,000 others were put out of action due to frostbite. Of the army's 3,200 troops who fought the CCF east of the reservoir, fewer than 400 survived. Chinese casualties were at least 40,000, perhaps much higher.

But other numbers attest to the success of the withdrawal. In more than one hundred ships, the navy evacuated 105,000 troops and 98,000 Korean refugees from the port of Hungnam. It also removed 17,500 vehicles and more than 350,000 tons of cargo. The evacuation's success, however, also demonstrated the failure of MacArthur's plan to end the war by Christmas and confirmed the folly of splitting his forces. Whether that mistake would be corrected, and corrected in time, would have to wait for the new year and a new commander for the Eighth Army.

Chapter 7

The Battle for Chipyong

A s the year 1951 began, the Korean War had become a very different conflict. The Chinese had entered the war and delivered stunning blows to the United Nations (UN) forces that had been confidently driving north in an effort to end the hostilities quickly. Now it was the Communist Chinese who were on the move, pushing south with the same outcome in mind. On New Year's Day, the Chinese Communist Forces (CCF) launched a new assault. They called it their Third Phase Offensive, and they put half a million troops in the field against the UN front line. The morale of the UN troops in the field was low, and the mood in Washington was gloomy.

But change was on the way. In fact, it had already begun with an unfortunate traffic accident.

Ridgway Takes Command

On December 23, 1950, General Walton Walker, commander of the Eighth U.S. Army in Korea, was on his way to inspect the troops at the front when his jeep was hit by a ROK truck. Walker was killed instantly. Three days later, General Matthew B. Ridgway was informed that he was the new commander of the Eighth Army. At the time of Walker's death, Ridgway was stationed in Washington as the deputy chief of staff for Operations and Administration of the army. Upon receiving word of his new assignment, Ridgway immediately made arrangements to go to Korea.

What he found when he arrived was disheartening, and the decorated World War II veteran knew he had a tough job ahead of him. He concluded, "Before the Eighth Army could return to the offensive it needed to have its fighting spirit restored, to have pride in itself, to feel confidence in its leadership, and to have faith in its mission."[76] Ridgway quickly set out to implement the improvements he felt were needed to get the Eighth Army in shape. For his eagerness to turn the army from retreating to attacking, he earned the nickname "Wrong-way Ridgway." But before his troops could advance, Ridgway knew that he had to stabilize his line, and that meant further withdrawal. For the second time in the war Seoul was abandoned, and the Eighth Army moved back to the Kum River in South Korea. To raise the morale of his troops, Ridgway wrote a message titled "Why Are We Here? What Are We Fighting For?" to be read to the entire Eighth Army. It stated, in part:

> We are here because of the decisions of the properly constituted authorities of our respective governments. . . . The issue now joined right here in Korea is whether communism or individual freedom shall prevail; whether the fight of fear-driven people we have witnessed here shall be checked, or shall at some future time, however distant, engulf our own loved ones in all its misery and despair. You will have my utmost. I shall expect yours.[77]

With the X Corps now part of the Eighth Army and with shortened supply lines delivering the ammunition and supplies needed by the frontline troops, Ridgway was about to undertake his first offensive since assuming command.

Crossroads

Situated about thirty miles east of Seoul, the town of Chipyong stood in a valley surrounded by eight high hills. Most of its buildings were made of mud and straw, with a few made of bricks or wood frame. Many of the structures had already been damaged or destroyed in earlier fighting. Southwest of the village was a small, newly constructed airstrip. But Chipyong's significance lay in what ran through the village: A single-track railroad and several

Lieutenant General Matthew B. Ridgway became commander of the Eighth Army after General Walker died in an automobile accident.

roads intersected at the town, leading to strategic points all across Korea. Thus, as a crossroads in the center of the country, Chipyong was important to both the UN and the Communist forces. From there the UN could effectively mount further counteroffensives; if the CCF controlled the town, they would be able to launch assaults of their own.

The Twenty-third Regimental Combat Team (RCT) arrived at Chipyong on February 3 and immediately formed a defensive perimeter around the town. Colonel Paul Freeman, commander of the RCT, had his orders from Ridgway: Hold the town against the Chinese. Knowing he had too few men to occupy the high hills, Free-

man deployed his infantry units, which included three U.S. battalions and a battalion of French troops, on low hills and in rice paddies closer to Chipyong. The perimeter surrounded the town in a rough rectangle about two and one-half miles long and between one and two miles wide. Freeman took the time to carefully prepare his defenses. "Inside the perimeter," an executive officer of a rifle company remembered, "we had some tanks and heavy mortars and an entire artillery battalion, about two dozen big guns. And we had an enormous supply of ammunition. Colonel Freeman had made sure of that."[78] Crews carefully aimed their artillery pieces at the areas most likely to be used by the CCF in

Ridgway: A Soldier's General

After the death of General Walton Walker in December 1950, the Eighth Army gained a new leader: General Matthew B. Ridgway. With Ridgway in charge, the morale of the UN forces in Korea rose and there was a renewed resolve among the troops to fight and defeat the enemy.

Matthew Bunker Ridgway was born in 1895 in Virginia and graduated from the U.S. Military Academy at West Point in 1917. After World War I, Ridgway was given several assignments in the United States and in Latin America (he spoke fluent Spanish). In World War II, he commanded the Eighty-second Airborne Division and parachuted with his troops in the D day invasion of Normandy. After taking command of the Eighth Army and restoring his men's morale and pride, Ridgway eventually replaced Douglas MacArthur as commander in chief of the UN forces in Korea.

Ridgway believed in his men, especially the humble foot soldier, and expressed his views in

his memoirs, as quoted in *Ridgway Duels for Korea* by Roy E. Appleman:

A commander must have far more concern for the welfare of his men than he has for his own safety. After all, the same dignity attaches to the mission given a single soldier as to the duties of the commanding general. The execution of the soldier's mission is just as vitally important, because it is the sum total of all these small individual missions, properly executed, which produces the results of the big unit. All lives are equal on the battlefield, and a dead rifleman is as great a loss, in the sight of God, as a dead general. The dignity which attaches to the individual is the basis of western civilization, and that fact should be remembered by every commander, platoon or army.

an assault. Freeman's men ran communication lines between the units, laid mines along the approaches to Chipyong, and established patrols outside the perimeter. "We patrolled extensively," recalled Freeman, "and we tried to give the impression that we were a much stronger force than just a regimental combat team."[79] Heavy mortars and fourteen tanks supported the infantry and artillery.

Despite all this careful preparation, Freeman knew that the odds against the Twenty-third RCT were not good. He had only about five thousand troops at Chipyong, including the French battalion and a company of Army Rangers. Although Freeman could only guess at the number of enemy troops facing him, he was certain that the Chinese were quietly massing an overwhelming force. In fact,

UN tanks helped Colonel Freeman's thin Twenty-third Regimental Combat Team (RCT) to fend off more than eighteen thousand CCF troops in the battle for Chipyong.

later accounts put the CCF strength at about eighteen thousand troops—more than three times the manpower assembled within the perimeter.

Observation flights over the Chipyong area had revealed enemy columns advancing toward the perimeter. Despite Ridgway's order to hold his position, Freeman knew that there was a real possibility that he could be cut off by the CCF. When he asked for permission to withdraw, he received a message from headquarters: "8th Army CG [Commanding General] has decided you stay where you are."[80] The best that Ridgway could do was to promise to send assistance as soon as possible, but Freeman realized that the Chinese would likely attack before help could arrive.

On the night of February 13, 1950, Freeman told his unit commanders, "We'll stay here and fight it out."[81] The men of the Twenty-third Regimental Combat Team nervously waited at their positions. And in the darkness outside the perimeter, the Chinese were closing in.

The Attack Begins

At around 8:00 P.M. the men of the Twenty-third heard bugles and whistles blowing, the traditional signal of an attack by Chinese forces. They couldn't see anything in the dark so they held their fire and waited. But no attack came, and the perimeter remained quiet. Then, just after 10:00 P.M., the Chinese assault against Chipyong began with a barrage of mortar and artillery fire coming from several directions.

One round struck an antiaircraft artillery vehicle inside the perimeter and set it on fire; another hit near the regimental command post. Soon other shells found their way into the perimeter, and Freeman recalled not having "received such a concentration of heavy weapons fire since the [battle of the] Naktong [Bulge]."[82]

At the northwest end of the perimeter, where Company C was dug in, CCF infantry advanced, tripping signal flares and running into antipersonnel mines. But still the men held their fire. They called on the artillery battery to fire 155mm illuminating shells, which would light up the battlefield and expose the advancing enemy. When the shells turned the nighttime battlefield into daylight, Company C opened fire with its machine guns. The French battalion, which was emplaced along the perimeter just west of Company C, joined in with its own automatic fire, and soon the first CCF attack was driven back.

After a short period of calm, the Chinese infantry renewed its assault, attacking Company A of the First Battalion along the north border of the perimeter. Further attacks came on the southeast of the line against Company K, and by 3:00 A.M. on February 14, the Chinese were attacking everywhere along the perimeter. Freeman countered the CCF assault with his whole arsenal: Along with the infantry's rifles and hand grenades, 155mm artillery pieces, machine guns, mortars, and tanks poured fire onto the advancing enemy. The Chinese suffered hundreds

Digging In

At Chipyong, as well as at many other battles during the Korean War, the bitter winter was often as tenacious an enemy as the North Koreans or the Chinese. One of the most basic defensive actions that a soldier can take is to dig a foxhole or other protective cover. Winters in Korea, however, seemed to conspire against such defenses, as Roy E. Appleman relates in his book *Ridgway Duels for Korea:*

> The 23rd RCT did not at first dig in much at Chipyong, but as the enemy buildup there developed and it finally appeared that a battle would be fought there, more attention was given to this need. American troops did not like to dig much, especially in frozen ground. The artillery batteries, however, did a good job of getting their guns dug in. The ground was frozen down to a depth of 8 to 10 inches. On top it was all pick work. A shovel would not make a dent in the ground until the hole had reached about 12 inches in depth. The artillerymen used a sledge to drive a crowbar into the frozen ground and then put a winch on it to pry a break in the ground. The infantry, in general, did not do a very good job of digging in. [I] walked around the perimeter of the UN forces at Chipyong in August 1951 and saw very few foxholes. . . . In some places loose rocks were piled up in low parapets at some infantry positions. The most dug-in positions were on G Company's hill, and many of them were made on its reverse slope by the Chinese when they got possession of the hill.

of casualties before withdrawing once more to regroup.

At the western side of the perimeter the French battalion was holding its own against the onslaught. The Chinese launched an attack on the French portion of the line with bugles blaring and whistles screaming. Unintimidated by the din, the French proceeded to deploy their own noisemaker: a hand-cranked siren. With the siren wailing, the French charged the enemy with their bayonets fixed to their rifles, throwing hand grenades as they ran. According to military historian Russell Gugeler, "When the two forces were within twenty yards of each other, the Chinese suddenly turned and ran in the opposite direction. It was all over within a minute."[83]

Day Two

By the morning of February 14, the Chinese troops had withdrawn into the hills, leaving Freeman to assess the situation at the Chipyong perimeter. "We had had a rough night but had not really been in grave danger at any point. No reserves had been committed and we had not suffered too many casualties."[84] Two hundred men had been wounded in the battle, and soon Freeman would be among them.

Just after daybreak a Chinese 120mm mortar shell landed in the perimeter and exploded near the regimental command post, wounding several officers, one mortally. A fragment from that same round struck Colonel Freeman in the left calf, causing a jagged wound and possibly breaking the leg bone. Despite his wound, Freeman refused to consider being evacuated while his troops were in combat. A medic bandaged the wound and Freeman continued with his duties, limping as he walked around the command post. When news of Freeman's wound reached X Corps headquarters, Colonel Jack Chiles was flown into the perimeter to take command of the Twenty-third. After much persuasion Freeman finally agreed to leave, but not until he could be sure his troops were safe: "I told Chiles to find a shelter and stay out of the way until my departure."[85]

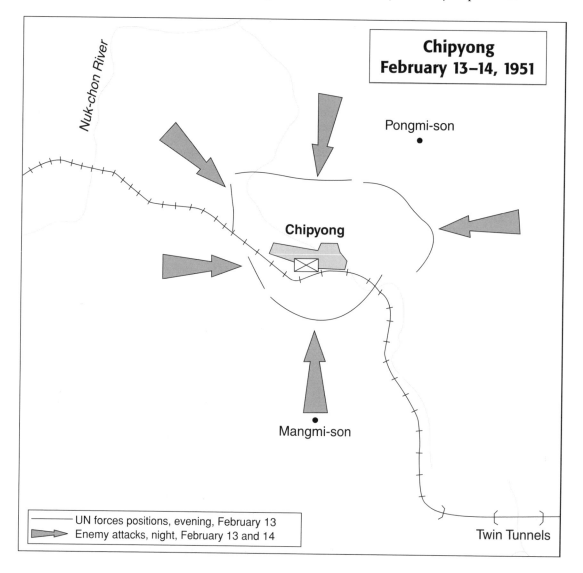

Chipyong
February 13–14, 1951

Nuk-chon River

Pongmi-son

Chipyong

Mangmi-son

Twin Tunnels

UN forces positions, evening, February 13
Enemy attacks, night, February 13 and 14

During the daylight hours on the fourteenth, men of the Twenty-third RCT kept busy preparing for the next attack, which would surely come by nightfall. "Good hot meals were served," recalled Freeman, "ammunition was distributed, weapons cleaned and readied, wires spliced, armored vehicles serviced, trip flares and mines reset."[86] Throughout the day the air force carried out air strikes with napalm on the Chinese positions in the hills surrounding Chipyong. Soldiers within the perimeter would watch as the "entire side or top of a hill would erupt in a big roiling ball of orange flame and thick black smoke."[87] Cargo aircraft dropped supplies to the troops, although some fell outside the perimeter and into Chinese hands.

As darkness fell on February 14, the CCF began probing attacks on the line, and by midnight the perimeter was once more fully engaged. The heaviest concentration of Chinese firepower was directed at the southern side of the perimeter where Company G was trying desperately to hold onto its hill. At one point, company commander Lieutenant Thomas Heath rallied his troops by shouting, "Get up on that hill. You'll die down here anyway. You might as well go up on the hill and die there."[88] After several hours of intense combat, during which Company G suffered numerous casualties, the Chinese were steadily gaining on the U.S. position. Using small arms and grenades, the Chinese fought the defenders in a foxhole-by-foxhole battle. At about 3:15

A.M. on February 15, Company G, with only a few men left, could hold on no longer and abandoned the hill to the enemy. It was the first CCF penetration of the Chipyong perimeter.

Any breach of the perimeter was serious, because it could serve as a gateway that the enemy could use to get to the interior of the defensive positions. If that happened, Chipyong would be lost. Quickly a platoon from Company F and one from the Ranger Company were dispatched to try to regain Company G's position. But the counterattack failed, and the Chinese, after nearly wiping out the two U.S. platoons, remained on the hill.

By daylight on the fifteenth, the Chinese were still attacking all along the perimeter, and Freeman had to put his last reserve troops into the fight. The outcome was looking more and more in doubt. But help was on the way.

Task Force Crombez

On February 14, as the fighting along the Chipyong perimeter intensified, a call went out to Colonel Marcel Crombez, commander of the Fifth Cavalry Regiment. General Bryant Moore, Crombez's superior, gave the Belgian-born colonel his orders: He was to assemble a task force and take it to Chipyong to rescue the surrounded Twenty-third RCT. "You'll have to move tonight," Moore said, "and I know you will do it."[89] The task force included infantry, combat engineers, and medics, plus medium Sherman and heavy Patton tanks,

American soldiers wait for dinner in the freezing cold at Chipyong. The brutal winter at Chipyong was as fierce an enemy as the Chinese or North Koreans.

self-propelled artillery pieces, and other armored vehicles. Crombez's force would travel north toward Chipyong along a narrow, icy road. The entire distance of about fifteen miles ran through dangerous, enemy-held territory.

Task Force Crombez moved out at nightfall on February 14, but after several miles the column was halted by a blown-out bridge. Engineers spent the night repairing the bridge, and, by the next morning, the force was moving again. But it was slow going because the infantry battalions were constantly harassed by fierce enemy fire. It soon became apparent that with the infantry bogged down in fighting off the enemy, the task force would not reach Chipyong by nightfall. Crombez decided to form an armored column that could break through the enemy fire and quickly reach the perimeter. The rest of the task force would follow as soon as possible. The armored column that Crombez assembled included 23 tanks with about 160 soldiers riding on them to provide defensive firepower.

At 3:45 P.M. on February 15, Colonel Crombez climbed into the fifth tank in line and the armored column moved out. It had not gone more than a few miles when it encountered mortar and small arms fire. "Near the small village of Koksu-ri," Crombez later recalled, "the Task Force came under intense enemy small arms fire, the tanks stopped, and some of the infantry were forced to dismount from the tanks." When the column halted, the tanks and infantrymen opened fire at the Chinese troops along the ridges that lined the road. After suppressing the enemy fire, the column started up again. For the next several hours casualties mounted as the task force moved steadily north, occasionally stopping to return enemy fire. The stretch of road between Koksu-ri and Chipyong presented the task force with some of its most vicious opposition. "The last 4 1/2 miles to Chipyong," Crombez said, "we encountered constant enemy fire, small arms, automatic weapons fire, mortar, bazooka 2.36 [inch] and some 3.5 fanatical Chinese attempted with pole and satchel charges to stop the tanks. The bow gunner in my tank killed off two 2.36 bazooka crews."[90]

As the tanks approached Chipyong, they had to navigate through a narrow pass where the road was bounded on each side by thirty- to fifty-foot-high ridges. By Crombez's estimate, about two thousand Chinese troops were waiting on the ridges for the column to approach. As the lead tank entered the pass, the CCF attacked with an all-out barrage of small arms fire, grenades, rockets, and satchel charges. Despite the intense enemy fire, each tank ran the gauntlet of the pass, and the entire column, minus one tank, made it through.

Saving the Twenty-Third

While the task force continued its advance, back at Chipyong the Chinese were still hammering at the south side of the perimeter. But the defenders held on and soon were able to mount an effective counterattack. Four tanks were sent down the road past the south side of the perimeter, with the task of going behind the Chinese and firing on them from the rear in an effort to take back Company G's position. At about 4:45 P.M. on February 15, the first tanks of Task Force Crombez approached the perimeter. Thinking the tanks ahead of them were the enemy's, Crombez was about to open fire on them when he realized they were American tanks. The U.S. tanks then cleared the way for the task force's armor, which entered the perimeter to the cheers of the exhausted defenders. A sergeant in the task force recalled that "some of the men of the 23d infantry

and some of the French trench troops came out and kissed my tank."[91]

By now the defenders on the south perimeter line finally had the Chinese on the run, and with the task force's tanks rumbling into Chipyong, enemy resistance was diminishing all along the perimeter. Soon the Chinese melted back into the hills, and the Chipyong perimeter was finally quiet. The Twenty-third Regimental Combat Team had been saved.

Engineers inspect a bridge destroyed by CCF troops. The bridge was repaired overnight, allowing Task Force Crombez to advance toward Chipyong.

But in the aftermath of the three-day siege, there were casualties to assess. The Twenty-third RCT lost 52 killed, 259 wounded, and 42 missing. Task Force Crombez sustained 71 casualties, including 12 killed. Although the exact number of Chinese casualties will never be known,

Slaughter at Chipyong

After the remnants of Company G abandoned their position to the enemy, other units tried to dislodge the Chinese from the hill. Lieutenant Lynn Freeman, the executive officer in a rifle company, describes one battle and its aftermath in *No Bugles, No Drums: An Oral History of the Korean War* by Rudy Tomedi:

> Finally we got the call, we were going to counterattack, and around the middle of the morning we moved out with the rest of the ranger company and tried to retake the hill where G Company's old positions were. As long as the Chinese held that hill they controlled part of our perimeter, and they could force a major breakthrough at any time.
>
> We made several attempts to get up there. Our starting point was a road and a patch of flat land. Then we had to move up a gradually rising slope that had practically no cover on it. We were getting hit with small arms fire, machine-gun fire, mortar fire, indirect fire from our own captured bazookas. It was murderous. There was a constant buzzing in the air from all the bullets. As officers we were trying to push our men forward, but the fire would get so intense that nobody could move. All the while we're firing our own weapons, and finally the ammo gets low and you've got to pull back. . . .
>
> We were still trying to take those positions when [Task Force Crombez] came up from the south, about four in the afternoon, and as their lead tanks approached the perimeter the Chinese withdrew. God, we were happy to see those guys. In fact, we cheered like hell.
>
> Afterward, I walked the perimeter, just looking around. I went down a little draw, and I'll never forget the sight. There were hundreds of burned bodies in it. The snow was burned off the ground and Chinese bodies were lying in heaps, all scorched and burned from our napalm, their arms and legs frozen in grotesque angles. Our air force had used a lot of napalm on them, and it is almost beyond belief the way they continued to fight in broad daylight, so exposed like that. But what I saw in that draw was only the beginning. We found hundreds and hundreds more, caught in the draws and ravines where they'd been trying to hide.
>
> I never saw such slaughter, before or since.

The body of a CCF soldier killed by U.S. Marine air support lies on a hillside.

estimates place CCF losses at around 5,000 killed or wounded.

The battle for Chipyong handed the CCF their first defeat of the Korean War and kept a strategic town out of their control. It gave a badly needed morale boost to the UN troops and provided a dramatic example of how a small but dedicated force can stand its ground against tremendous odds. Colonel Freeman was understandably proud of his men. He wrote to them in a farewell letter, "Offi-

cers and men, I want to say to you that there is no grander fighting regiment in all the world than the 23d RCT. . . . God Bless you all."[92]

The Korean War was about to undergo a change in strategy that would last for the remainder of the conflict. The fierce fighting of the first year would grind to a standstill, with each side gaining little ground as they battled for control of the rocky hills that dotted the Korean landscape.

✮ Chapter 8 ✮

Stalemate: The Battle of Pork Chop Hill

At the dawn of the new year 1953, the United Nations (UN) Command had been engaged in a fierce struggle against the Communist North Korean and Chinese forces in Korea for two and one-half years. After the first year of combat, during which the two sides fought a bloody seesaw battle for control of the Korean peninsula, the conflict had bogged down into a stalemate. UN and Communist troops dug in and confronted each other in a series of intense skirmishes in the hills and ridges along a static battlefront. Neither side made lasting progress. A hill might be captured one day, only to be lost to the enemy the next. As often as not, the same hill would change hands several times.

One hill that saw such back-and-forth fighting in the last year of the war appeared on UN maps simply as "Hill 255." But despite its prosaic military designation, Hill 255 became not only a symbol of the stalemate that existed in Korea, but also a political pawn in the larger game of peace negotiations. Back home in the United States, few people would have recognized the name Hill 255. They knew it by a name that would become famous in the years after the war: Pork Chop Hill.

The Outpost War

By the spring of 1951, forward progress by either side in the war had virtually ceased. What had been a war of maneuver had become a stalemate along a stationary front known as the Main Line of Resistance (MLR). The MLR was a crooked line that stretched across the Korean peninsula from the Imjin River in the west to the Sea of Japan in the east— a total of more than 150 miles. It was located a few miles north of the 38th parallel, the original boundary between North and South Korea.

All along the MLR both sides dug trenches to protect their troops. Underground bunkers were constructed to provide secure space for storing supplies and for eating and sleeping. On the UN side, emplaced ahead of these trenches in a line running roughly parallel to the MLR was a series of fortified hills and ridges called combat outposts. Almost all the combat during the last two years of the Korean War centered on these outposts, thus giving this phase of the conflict the name "outpost war." Fortified with sandbags and barbed wire, the combat outposts served as observation and early warning posts and as jumping-off points for patrols into enemy territory. Despite the lack of movement on the front line, the outpost war added thousands of casualties to the total of dead, wounded, and missing in the Korean War.

U.S. Marines take cover in a trench during intense fighting. Along the Main Line of Resistance (MLR), both sides dug into trenches to protect their troops.

Life on Pork Chop

S.L.A. Marshall depicts the scene just before the first engagement with the Chinese in his book *Pork Chop Hill*:

Had [the outguards in front of Pork Chop Hill] talked, it might have been about the weather, for now the Korean spring was at its best. The slopes of their battlement were fragrant from the profusion of wild plums and chindolea blossoms. The air was balmy. A cloudless day was giving way to a starlit night. The pall of smoke, arising from numerous forest fires, and dressing the far horizon, was the only reminder that the season had been excessively dry.

Despite its incongruity with the other parts of the main defensive line, Pork Chop in itself was a snug position. The little hill had been engineered according to the pattern then conventional with Eighth Army. It was a buffer intended to break up the Chinese attack before it could violate the main line. A solidly revetted rifle trench encircled it at the military crest, providing wall and some roof cover, which served for defense in any direction. Sandbagged and heavily timbered, fire-slotted bunkers were tied into the trench line at approximately 30-yard intervals. They gave troops protection while affording observation and command of the slope. These were stout, unblemished works. They had recently been overhauled and fire had not yet mauled them.

The top of Pork Chop was pushed in, like the dent in the crown of a hat. In consequence, its works could not form an evenly rounded perimeter. The dent was on the rearward side of the hill. The draw, reaching to the crest, in effect produced a divided perimeter. The two platoons were loosely joined in the center. But the odd shape of the hill nonetheless put them in separate compartments.

One of these outposts was Hill 255. On military maps, each significant Korean hill was given a number corresponding to its height in meters. But when viewed from the air, Hill 255 looked like a giant pork chop. The Americans picked up on the unusual shape, and the nickname stuck. It was a frivolous name for a hill that would see so much bloodshed so close to the end of the war.

Negotiating for Peace

With their casualties mounting at a horrifying rate, Chinese leaders were becoming increasingly convinced that they could not win the war on the battlefield. The Soviet Union also put pressure on China and North Korea to come to the bargaining table. On July 10, 1951, peace negotiations began in the North Korean town of Kaesong, not far from the MLR. Harassment by North Korean troops forced the negotiators to transfer the talks in October to a safer location in the town of Panmunjom. They would remain there for the duration of the negotiations.

While the peace talks dragged on in the truce tent, on the battlefield the killing continued. The outposts around which the battles raged were, from a strategic standpoint, virtually worthless. But now the political significance of the fighting had relegated strategic matters to the background. To test UN resolve at critical moments at the bargaining table, the Communists would turn up the heat on the battlefield. Any ground gained by the Communists, no matter how small, would add to the territory possessed by North Korea after an armistice was signed. It was equally important for the UN to hold onto its territory. By fighting to maintain the positions it had won at such a high cost, the UN was showing the Communists that it could not be intimi-dated on the battlefield, and that such determination would extend to the peace negotiations as well.

"Take Good Care of Our Pork Chop"

By May 1952 the Eighth Army had five corps stretching the width of the Korean peninsula to oppose the Chinese and North Korean People's Army (NKPA) forces. In all, nearly a quarter of a million

North Korean and UN negotiators bargain over a map of Korea during peace talks at Panmunjom.

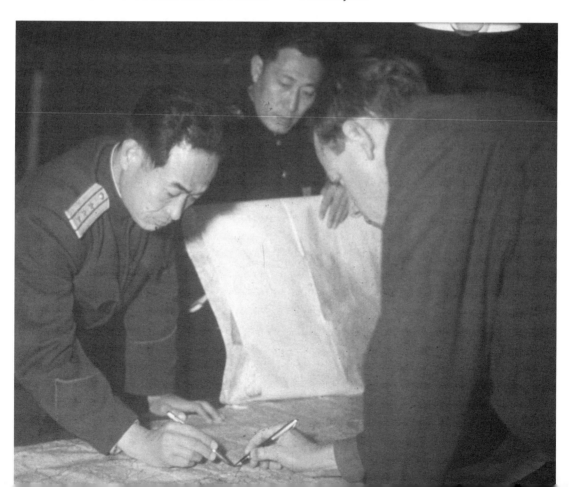

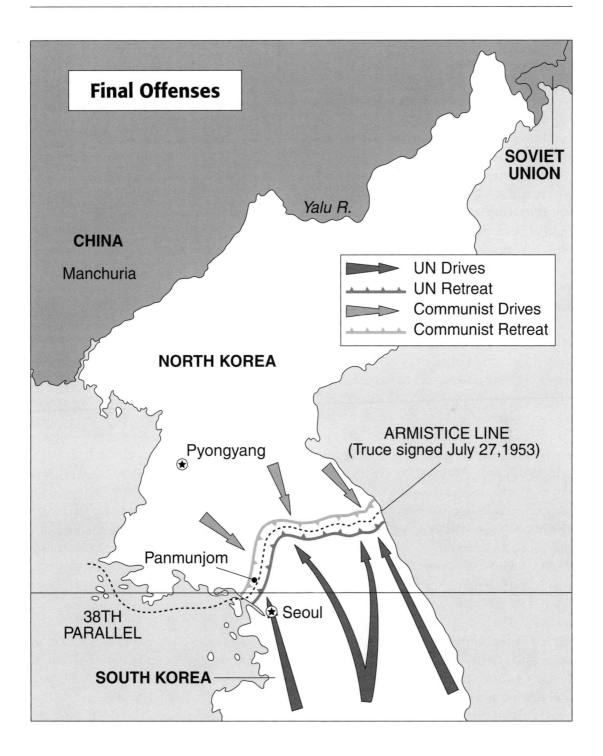

Final Offenses

SOVIET
UNION

Yalu R.

CHINA

Manchuria

→	UN Drives
→	UN Retreat
→	Communist Drives
→	Communist Retreat

NORTH KOREA

ARMISTICE LINE
(Truce signed July 27, 1953)

⭐ Pyongyang

Panmunjom

38TH
PARALLEL

⭐ Seoul

SOUTH KOREA

UN frontline troops opposed 291,000 Communist soldiers along the MLR. In early June, the UN and Communist forces were engaged in fierce fighting near the town of Chorwon. Coming under heavy Communist artillery fire, UN troops carried out assaults on enemy hilltop positions. I Corps's plan was to capture about a dozen hills forward of the MLR, including Pork Chop Hill. During two days of fighting for control of the hills on June 6 and 7, Pork Chop Hill, which was occupied by soldiers of the Chinese 116th Division, was captured by elements of the 180th Infantry Regiment of the Forty-fifth Infantry Division. Several Chinese Communist Forces (CCF) counterattacks were driven back, and Pork Chop Hill remained firmly in UN possession. Troops began fortifying the hilltop with sandbags and barbed wire. A nearby hill named Old Baldy was also captured.

Several different UN forces maintained control of Pork Chop Hill in the fall of 1952 as units were rotated to other assignments. When the Second Infantry Division replaced the Forty-fifth, troops of the Ninth Regiment took over Pork Chop and Old Baldy. In November, the Twenty-first Infantry Regiment from Thailand defended the hill against several Communist assaults. When the Thai regiment was replaced by the Thirty-first Regiment of the Seventh Infantry Division, the new defenders found a message scrawled on the wall of a bunker on Pork Chop Hill: "Take good care of our Pork Chop." Although

UN forces thus far had managed to ward off Chinese attempts to take Pork Chop Hill, it would become increasingly difficult to do so in the months ahead.

The First Assault

By early 1953, the Chinese were becoming more aggressive in their assaults on the MLR. At the beginning of March, the Chinese staged an artillery barrage against Pork Chop Hill and its neighbor Old Baldy, firing some eight thousand shells against the UN fortifications that topped the hills. Then, after a three-week lull, Chinese infantry launched a ground assault on the two hills. Corporal Joe Scheuber recalled the action:

> On March 23rd, we ran a 50-man patrol along the perimeter of Pork Chop. We just got into our foxholes on the finger of Pork Chop when enemy mortar and artillery hit us. To our right, more incoming rounds. Then we saw Chinese behind us and realized we were surrounded. We fell back to the trench line at the top of the hill, but the Chinese had reached it first. Hand-to-hand fighting broke out. There was a tremendous amount of noise. I got nicked in the arm and my helmet fell off. . . . I ended up in a shell hole the remainder of the night, as the enemy artillery lasted most of the night. When dawn broke I was found by another unit from I Company as they pushed the Chinese off the hill.[93]

While Pork Chop Hill remained in UN hands, the fighting continued on Old Baldy. Defending the hill was an inexperienced Colombian battalion that had just recently arrived in Korea. The Chinese began their attack by pounding the hill with heavy artillery fire. Before long it became obvious that, even with American reinforcements, the Colombians were no match for the veteran CCF troops. Old Baldy ultimately fell to the Communists.

Plans for a counterattack to regain the hill were soon under way. But then General Maxwell Taylor, who had assumed command of the Eighth Army in February, tallied up the casualties his force had suffered so far: three hundred killed, wounded, or missing. Deciding that Old

A Taste for Battle

Joe Scheuber, a corporal in the Seventh Division, relates his personal story of fighting on Pork Chop Hill in the book *The Korean War: Uncertain Victory: An Oral History* by Donald Knox and Alfred Coppel:

> We were loaded into trucks and taken as near to the "finger" of Porkchop as possible without being observed by the enemy. We got out of the trucks with our gear and weapons and were warned to be alert—which meant that the enemy had to be close by. I carried an M1 rifle, three grenades, and as much ammo as I could beg or borrow. If I had known what was coming, I would have loaded up with grenades. . . . We had no more than taken cover when enemy mortar and artillery started falling all around us. It was dark, and the flashes lit up the night.

One of Scheuber's comrades, a Browning automatic rifle (BAR) man, was wounded in the shelling, so Scheuber picked up his weapon.

> I tried to work the BAR but it was jammed. Someone else had a radio, but it didn't work. Off to the right we could see the flashes of incoming artillery landing. There were columns of Chinese moving. Then we saw that there were Chinese behind us as well. We were surrounded. . . .

> The fighting was heavy and confused. I turned to look back, hoping that some more of our people might be coming up to reinforce us. As I did, an enemy soldier shot my steel helmet off my head. I hit the ground and lost my rifle. I grabbed a grenade and threw it, never hearing it explode, though it must have. I saw the Korean soldier that had been with me in the foxhole run his bayonet into a Chinese. There was a tremendous amount of noise and confusion, with bullets flying in every direction. It looked to me as though we were being pushed off the hill. A bullet tugged at my field jacket and nicked my arm. I got up and started back down the hill. As I did that, I caught sight of a Chinese soldier shooting at me. I lobbed a grenade at him and killed him.

> Then, quite suddenly, I found myself in a foxhole—a shallow one—holding my last grenade with the pin pulled. I tried to think what I would do if the Chinese came upon me. Would I throw the grenade—my last weapon of any sort—or would I blow myself up and hope to take one of them with me? Among the many things that crossed my mind in those moments was the question, What in hell was I, an American, doing here, in Korea, fighting Chinese?

Baldy was not important enough to expend any more lives, Maxwell ordered his troops not to counterattack.

After the Chinese captured Old Baldy, Pork Chop seemed destined to become the next to fall. After all, if Taylor wanted to save lives by giving up Old Baldy, the same logic could have applied to Pork Chop as well. But politics now began to play a role in the outpost war. According to military historian S.L.A. Marshall, conceding Pork Chop to the enemy would have made some military sense, but "national pride, bruised by the enemy's rudeness toward Old Baldy, asserted itself, and Pork Chop was held.[94]

Easy Company

After the assaults on the Pork Chop–Old Baldy area in March, there was a break in the action around Pork Chop Hill for several weeks while the Chinese took their battles to other places along the MLR. But they had not forgotten about Pork Chop and were busy resupplying for another try at capturing the hill. On several occasions in early April, UN patrols encountered small groups of Chinese soldiers probing for weak spots in Pork Chop Hill's defenses. The UN and Chinese troops engaged in brief skirmishes that left several casualties on both sides.

The defense of Pork Chop Hill fell to Company E, Thirty-first Regiment of the Seventh Infantry Division. Although companies were designated by a letter, for clarity in radio transmissions they were referred to using the military phonetic alphabet. Company A was Able, Company B was Baker, and so on. Company E was called Easy Company, but there would be nothing easy about its task because at ninety-six men it was an understrength unit. This total, including seventy-six riflemen of the First and Third Platoons, plus artillery, engineering, and medical personnel, was only about half of the men the company normally fielded. "Worse yet," wrote S.L.A. Marshall, "not all of [the riflemen] were available to man the main rampart. Twenty had been paired off for duty as outguards. After dark, they would descend to ten listening posts which formed a crescent around the lower forward and flank slopes of the hill. There they would await any approach by the enemy, hoping to sound the alarm and then duck back."[95]

Lieutenant Thomas V. Harrold, commander of Easy Company, had received intelligence reports that the Chinese were planning a major assault on Pork Chop, probably on April 16. After passing the word to his subordinates, Harrold was confident that his men would be prepared for the attack. Only later would he learn that many of his men, including the outguards, did not receive the message and that no special precautions were being taken for the night of April 16.

Red Stars in the Sky

At about 11:00 P.M., a patrol encountered a small force of some fifty Chinese troops that had entered the area from nearby

Hasakkol ridge. In the ensuing firefight, the U.S. troops attempted to drive the enemy back with grenades. But soon the patrol's withdrawal route was cut off, and they had to remain dug in until they could make it back to Pork Chop the next day. Communications between the patrol and Pork Chop Hill had been cut, so no one on the hill knew of the patrol's skirmish.

At about the same time, a barrage of Chinese artillery fire began falling on Pork Chop Hill. Harrold quickly told two other lieutenants to call the outguards and tell them to withdraw, but with communications out, there was no response from outside the perimeter. Then he fired a red star rocket into the air over Pork Chop Hill, the signal that his position was under attack. A few seconds later Harrold fired another flare, a red star cluster that meant "Give us flash Pork Chop," a request for artillery fire. The answer to his

Gregory Peck calls for reinforcements in this scene from the 1959 movie Pork Chop Hill.

Music on Pork Chop Hill

Surrounded by darkness and an unseen enemy, the troops on Pork Chop Hill could be forgiven if they were a bit unsettled by their surroundings. Strange music, coming from somewhere out in the night, added to the disconcerting atmosphere. In his book *Pork Chop Hill*, military historian S.L.A. Marshall describes an eerie evening on the hill:

> From the superior height of the enemy-held ridge named Hasakkol, the light breeze of early evening brought to Pork Chop Hill the sound of music.

> For some minutes it continued, rising, then fading out according to the caprice of the wind. Men were singing in chorus. It was a mournful chanting, faint, tremulous and uncanny. And though the voices were high-pitched, there was a muted quality to the music, as if it came out of a deep well. Now it became lost in distance again and the men who had paused to listen resumed their supper of steak, French fries and chocolate ice cream.

> A private said, "It sounds like they're gathering in the tunnels."

> Another answered, "O.K., as long as they stay there."

Asked the lieutenant, "But what does it mean?"

"They're prayer singing," said the interpreter. "I can't hear the words but I know the music. They're getting ready to die."

In this manner, Lieut. Thomas V. Harrold got his first pointed warning that his men, Easy Company of the 31st Regiment, and their home of the moment, Pork Chop Hill, had been marked for special attention by the Communist Chinese.

Until then, his concern about this particular night had not been deeply personal. For more than a week, the report had been circulating in the division that the enemy would make an attack in main at 2300 [11:00 P.M.] on 16 April. . . . On hearing it from G2 [Intelligence] Harrold had felt no special alarm. The report said the blow would fall farther east along the division front. In the past there had been several such rumors, which had never materialized.

But the music from Hasakkol was like a gun pointing at Harrold's head. If Pork Chop was to be a main target, its commander of the moment had reason to reflect that his situation, and the circumstances of his company, were not bright with promise.

signals came just two minutes later in a burst of artillery fire, the UN's answer to the Chinese barrage. The artillery duel lasted about twenty minutes, after which the hill became quiet.

But the Chinese had already infiltrated Pork Chop's trenches, and grenade and small arms fire broke out along the perimeter. Casualties mounted, and calls for help went out to UN units on neighboring hills;

but the Chinese steadily advanced, and by 2:00 A.M. on April 17, they had taken most of Pork Chop Hill. The remaining men of Easy Company held on to what little portions of the hill they still occupied, engaging in close-quarters combat with the Chinese. As the battle continued and reinforcements began to arrive, two platoons from King Company and Love Company were ordered to prepare a counterattack on the hill. Lieutenant Joseph Clemons, commander of King Company, gave orders to his platoon leaders: "Hit the hill hard and get to the top as fast as the men can go. Success depends on speed; we must close before daylight."[96] It was tough going for the men of King Company. "Pork Chop was steep," recalled a sergeant. "We were heavily loaded with ammo for our weapons and the MGs [machine guns], as well as the boxes of grenades. The steep climb had us pooped."[97] Just as they reached the hill's defenses at about 5:00 A.M., the Chinese began shelling Pork Chop again.

Love Company attacked at about the same time as King Company but was driven back by the Chinese barrage. Not until dawn on April 17 did the men of King and Love Companies finally reach the survivors of Easy Company, who had taken refuge in bunkers on the hill. Now only fifty-five men from Easy, King, and Love Companies remained on Pork Chop Hill to fight off the Chinese.

The Seventeenth Takes Over

Throughout the next day, the small group of defenders held their ground on Pork Chop Hill. The Chinese had taken cover in Pork Chop's trenches and were engaging the tiny defending force in hand-to-hand combat. Chinese reinforcements began arriving on Pork Chop from Hasakkol to augment the attacking force, but soon UN air and artillery strikes had them pinned down. The Chinese were not the only ones to receive reinforcements,

however. At about 8:15 A.M., elements of George Company, Seventeenth Infantry Regiment, began arriving on Pork Chop to help Easy, King, and Love Companies fight off the Chinese. The ferocity of the struggle for possession of Pork Chop Hill is illustrated by a radio message sent by Lieutenant Clemons to his battalion's headquarters: "I must have water, plasma, more medical assistance, flamethrowers, litter[s], ammunition, several radios."[98]

At noon on April 17, a message was sent to the hill that all units except what remained of King and Love Companies were ordered to withdraw from Pork Chop Hill. Clemons reported back that his small force would not be able to hold the hill without more reinforcements. Receiving no reply, Clemons began withdrawing his men. As the situation became more desperate, the question of how many men the UN Command was prepared to lose in order to retain Pork Chop Hill was being debated at Eighth Army headquarters. General Arthur Trudeau, Seventh Division commander, flew to Pork Chop by helicopter to get a firsthand look at the situation. By this time, about 3:00 P.M., the Pork Chop defending force was down to around twenty-five men. The decision was finally made that Pork Chop should be held and that Seventeenth Regiment of the Seventh Division would take over its defense.

Fox Company of the Seventeenth Regiment fought its way up the hill to the command post occupied by the remnants of King and Love Companies. By

The North Korean and Chinese cease-fire team poses previous to attending a peace conference.

midnight, the weary defenders had departed for the rear, leaving Fox to defend Pork Chop. Losing no time, Chinese troops surrounded the command post, mounted the roof, and dropped hand grenades into the bunker. UN artillery fire was called in to rid the crest of the hill of Chinese troops. It was mass confusion on Pork Chop Hill as artillery and mortar rounds exploded, machine gun fire raked the hill, and Fox Company engaged the enemy in hand-to-hand combat. Fox Company knew it could not withstand another Chinese assault.

Gain and Loss

At around 2:30 A.M. on April 18, Pork Chop Hill suddenly grew quiet. Then came the sounds of rifle fire signaling

that another Easy Company, this one from the Seventeenth Regiment, was attacking the Chinese as the Americans made their way up Pork Chop Hill. By taking a different route up the hill, Easy Company was able to avoid enemy artillery fire. Then, climbing steadily behind a "walking wall" of friendly artillery fire, it began pushing the Chinese troops back. But the Chinese fought back hard. It took the addition of Able Company, which had been waiting in reserve, to finally drive the Chinese from Pork Chop Hill. Finally, by the evening of April 18, UN forces were back in control. As historian Marshall said, "After sunset, the enemy gave over, Pork Chop became tranquil, the smoke blew away and men could see the stars once more."[99] The battle for Pork Chop Hill was over.

Or was it? During the months that followed the Chinese withdrawal from Pork Chop Hill, the CCF continued to assault the hill with artillery and mortar fire from the surrounding hills. Meanwhile, at the peace talks in Panmunjom, the terms for an armistice were almost settled when negotiations stalled over prisoners of war, a topic of contention throughout the talks. The Chinese took advantage of this pause to mount a last-ditch effort to claim Pork Chop Hill as their territory before the peace treaty was finalized. Renewed Chi-

nese assaults against Pork Chop Hill began on July 6, 1953, when CCF infantry stormed the hill after a preliminary artillery barrage. For days the battle seesawed back and forth as both sides fed reinforcements into the struggle to force the other off the hill. In the end, the UN forces realized that the Chinese were willing to sacrifice an unlimited number of men to gain the hill. So the UN commanders ordered Pork Chop Hill abandoned. On July 11 Pork Chop's gallant defenders were evacuated in armored personnel carriers, vehicles that normally delivered

General Mark W. Clark (left) signs an armistice in 1953 ending the three-year conflict in Korea.

food and ammunition to the front. This ruse fooled the Chinese, who were not aware that Pork Chop had been abandoned until two days later. When they finally charged up the hill to secure it, they ran into booby traps left behind by the UN defenders, a parting shot to the new tenants of the hill.

On July 27, 1953, less than two weeks after the fall of Pork Chop Hill to the Chinese, delegates in Panmunjom signed an armistice agreement ending the Korean War. Pork Chop Hill ended up partly in North Korea and partly in the Demilitarized Zone (DMZ), a "no-man's land" established between North and South Korea. A small hill of little military value, Pork Chop Hill became known not only for intense infantry combat but for the ar-

tillery bombardment that raged during the battle. In the first action, from April 16 through 18, UN artillery batteries fired more than seventy-seven thousand rounds —a record for such a small battlefront. S.L.A. Marshall recalled walking along the scarred hill shortly after the battle: "Pork Chop when the fight was over was as clean picked as Old Baldy. And its cratered slopes will not soon bloom again, for they are too well planted with rusty shards and empty tins and bones."[100] Those bones were reminders of the human cost of defending Pork Chop Hill. The UN Command suffered some three hundred casualties, a high price to pay for a tiny patch of land that, in the end, made no difference in the outcome of the Korean War.

☆ Notes ☆

Chapter 1: Conflict in Korea

1. Quoted in David McCullough, *Truman.* New York: Touchstone, 1992, pp. 775–6.

2. Quoted in McCullough, *Truman*, p. 780.

3. Matthew B. Ridgway, *The Korean War: How We Met the Challenge, How All-Out Asian War Was Averted, Why MacArthur Was Dismissed, Why Today's War Objectives Must Be Limited.* Garden City, NY: Doubleday, 1967, pp. 150, 151.

4. Quoted in John Toland, *In Mortal Combat.* New York: William Morrow, 1991, p. 481.

5. Quoted in Joseph C. Goulden, *Korea: The Untold Story of the Korean War.* New York: Times Books, 1982, p. 635.

6. Quoted in Goulden, *Korea*, p. 639.

7. Quoted in Bevin Alexander, *Korea: The First War We Lost.* New York: Hippocrene Books, 1987, p. 481.

Chapter 2: Task Force Smith: First Blood

8. Quoted in Rudy Tomedi, *No Bugles, No Drums: An Oral History of the Korean War.* New York: John Wiley, 1993, p. 1.

9. Quoted in Tomedi, *No Bugles, No Drums*, p. 2.

10. Douglas MacArthur, *Reminiscences.* New York: McGraw-Hill, 1964, p. 334.

11. Quoted in Roy E. Appleman, *South to the Naktong, North to the Yalu.* Washington, DC: Center of Military History, 1992, p. 60.

12. MacArthur, *Reminiscences*, p. 336.

13. Quoted in Tomedi, *No Bugles, No Drums*, p. 4.

14. Quoted in Appleman, *South to the Naktong, North to the Yalu*, p. 65.

15. Quoted in Donald Knox, *The Korean War: Pusan to Chosin: An Oral History.* San Diego: Harcourt Brace Jovanovich, 1985, p. 10.

16. Quoted in Tomedi, *No Bugles, No Drums*, p. 4.

17. Quoted in Tomedi, *No Bugles, No Drums*, p. 5.

18. Quoted in T.R. Fehrenbach, *This Kind of War: The Classic Korean War History.* Washington, DC: Brassey's, 1998, p. 69.

19. Quoted in Tomedi, *No Bugles, No Drums*, pp. 11–12.

20. Quoted in Goulden, *Korea*, p. 123.

21. Quoted in Goulden, *Korea*, p. 123.

22. Quoted in Knox, *The Korean War*, p. 23.

23. Quoted in Tomedi, *No Bugles, No Drums*, p. 8.

24. Quoted in Tomedi, *No Bugles, No Drums*, p. 8.

Chapter 3: The Landing at Inchon

25. Quoted in Curtis A. Utz, *Assault from the Sea: The Amphibious Landing at Inchon.* Washington, DC: Naval Historical Center, Department of the Navy, 1994, p. 16.

26. Quoted in Stanley Weintraub, *MacArthur's War: Korea and the Undoing of an American Hero.* New York: Free Press, 2000, p. 116.

27. MacArthur, *Reminiscences*, pp. 349–350.

28. MacArthur, *Reminiscences*, p. 352.

29. Quoted in Goulden, *Korea*, p. 206.

30. Quoted in Utz, *Assault from the Sea*, p. 27.

31. Quoted in Knox, *The Korean War*, p. 227.

32. Quoted in *Time*, "War in Asia," September 25, 1950, p. 28.

33. Quoted in Knox, *The Korean War*, p. 229.

34. Quoted in *Time*, "War in Asia," p. 28.

35. Quoted in Knox, *The Korean War*, p. 229.

36. MacArthur, *Reminiscences*, p. 353.

37. Quoted in Utz, *Assault from the Sea*, p. 29.

38. Quoted in *Time*, "War in Asia," p. 29.

39. Quoted in *Time*, "War in Asia," p. 29.

40. Quoted in Goulden, *Korea*, p. 215.

41. Quoted in Utz, *Assault from the Sea*, p. 38.

42. Quoted in Fehrenbach, *This Kind of War*, p. 167.

Chapter 4: Defending the Pusan Perimeter

43. Quoted in Tomedi, *No Bugles, No Drums*, p. 20.

44. Quoted in Goulden, *Korea*, p. 165.

45. Quoted in Knox, *The Korean War*, pp. 72–73.

46. Quoted in Knox, *The Korean War*, p. 73.

47. Quoted in Tomedi, *No Bugles, No Drums*, p. 20.

48. Quoted in Knox, *The Korean War*, p. 108.

49. Quoted in Goulden, *Korea*, p. 177.

Chapter 5: Unsan: China Enters the War

50. Quoted in Clay Blair, *The Forgotten War: America in Korea, 1950–1953.* New York: Times Books, 1987, p. 348.

51. Quoted in Edwin P. Hoyt, *The Day the Chinese Attacked: Korea, 1950.* New York: McGraw-Hill, 1990, p. 80–1.

52. Harry S. Truman, *Memoirs by Harry S. Truman*, vol. Two, *Years of Trial and Hope.* Garden City, NY: Doubleday, 1956, p. 360.

53. Quoted in Appleman, *South to the Naktong, North to the Yalu*, p. 608.

54. Quoted in Appleman, *South to the Naktong, North to the Yalu*, p. 669.

55. Quoted in Patrick C. Roe, *The Dragon Strikes: China and the Korean War: June–December 1950*. Novato, CA: Presidio Press, 2000, p. 175.

56. Appleman, *South to the Naktong, North to the Yalu*, p. 770.

57. Quoted in Blair, *The Forgotten War*, p. 337.

58. Quoted in Appleman, *South to the Naktong, North to the Yalu*, p. 677.

59. Quoted in Alexander, *Korea*, p. 270.

60. Quoted in Appleman, *South to the Naktong, North to the Yalu*, pp. 701–702.

61. Quoted in Knox, *The Korean War*, p. 437.

Chapter 6: Escape from the Chosin Reservoir

62. Quoted in William Manchester, *American Caesar: Douglas MacArthur 1880–1964*. Boston: Little, Brown, 1978, pp. 601, 604.

63. Quoted in Blair, *The Forgotten War*, p. 433.

64. Quoted in Martin Russ, *Breakout: The Chosin Reservoir Campaign, Korea 1950*. New York: Penguin Books, 1999, p. 74.

65. Quoted in Robert J. Dvorchak, *Battle for Korea: A History of the Korean Conflict*. Fiftieth Anniversary Edition. Conshohocken, PA: Combined Publishing, 2000, p. 124.

66. Quoted in Dvorchak, *Battle for Korea*, pp. 127–28.

67. Quoted in B. Gordon Wheeler, "Chosin Reservoir: Saga of Epic Heroism," *VFW Magazine*, December, 2000.

68. Quoted in Eric Hammel, *Chosin: Heroic Ordeal of the Korean War*. New York: Vanguard Press, 1981, p. 215.

69. Quoted in Russ, *Breakout*, p. 284.

70. Quoted in Russ, *Breakout*, p. 287.

71. Quoted in Russ, *Breakout*, p. 355.

72. Quoted in Blair, *The Forgotten War*, p. 537.

73. Quoted in Wheeler, "Chosin Reservoir".

74. Quoted in Dvorchak, *Battle for Korea*, p. 154.

75. Quoted in Dvorchak, *Battle for Korea*, p. 154.

Chapter 7: The Battle for Chipyong

76. Ridgway, *The Korean War*, p. 85.

77. Quoted in Dvorchak, *Battle for Korea*, pp. 174, 175.

78. Quoted in Tomedi, *No Bugles, No Drums*, p. 118.

79. Quoted in J.D. Coleman, *Wonju: The Gettysburg of the Korean War*. Washington, DC: Brassey's, 2000, p. 185.

80. Roy E. Appleman, *Ridgway Duels for Korea*. College Station: Texas A&M University Press, 1990, p. 258.

81. Quoted in Blair, *The Forgotten War,* p. 697.

82. Quoted in Blair, *The Forgotten War,* p. 698.

83. Quoted in Blair, *The Forgotten War,* p. 699.

84. Quoted in Blair, *The Forgotten War,* p. 699.

85. Quoted in Blair, *The Forgotten War,* p. 700.

86. Quoted in Blair, *The Forgotten War,* p. 700.

87. Quoted in Tomedi, *No Bugles, No Drums,* p. 119.

88. Quoted in Dvorchak, *Battle for Korea,* p. 184.

89. Quoted in Appleman, *Ridgway Duels for Korea,* p. 277.

90. Quoted in Appleman, *Ridgway Duels for Korea,* pp. 280, 282.

91. Quoted in Appleman, *Ridgway Duels for Korea,* p. 283.

92. Quoted in Toland, *In Mortal Combat,* p. 406.

Chapter 8: Stalemate: The Battle of Pork Chop Hill

93. Quoted in James I. Marino, "Meat Grinder on Pork Chop Hill," *Military History,* April 2003, p. 45.

94. S.L.A. Marshall, *Pork Chop Hill.* New York: William Morrow, 1956, p. 115.

95. Marshall, *Pork Chop Hill,* p. 117.

96. Quoted in Marino, "Meat Grinder on Pork Chop Hill," p. 46.

97. Quoted in Marino, "Meat Grinder on Pork Chop Hill," p. 46.

98. Quoted in Marino, "Meat Grinder on Pork Chop Hill," p. 47.

99. Marshall, *Pork Chop Hill,* p. 195.

100. Marshall, *Pork Chop Hill,* p. 197.

⋆ For Further Reading ⋆

Books

Deborah Bachrach, *The Korean War*. San Diego: Lucent Books, 1991. A comprehensive history of the Korean War, fully illustrated with photographs and maps.

Sonia G. Benson, *Korean War: Almanac and Primary Sources*. Detroit: U·X·L, 2002. This book covers the Korean War in detail, including its major battles. Material from twelve primary source documents such as oral histories, memoirs, and other sources are included.

———, *Korean War: Biographies*. Detroit: U·X·L, 2002. A companion to Benson's history, this volume profiles twenty-five people who played political or military roles in the Korean War. Included are military leaders of the war, including Douglas MacArthur, William F. Dean, Matthew B. Ridgway, and Walton H. Walker.

Maurice Isserman, *The Korean War*. New York: Facts On File, 1992. A straightforward history of the Korean War. Includes black-and-white photographs and a bibliography.

S.L.A. Marshall, *The Military History of the Korean War*. New York: Franklin Watts, 1963. A short but classic work centering on the military action of the Korean War. The author is a retired brigadier general and military historian.

Websites

The Cold War, Episode 5: Korea (http://www.cnn.com/SPECIALS/cold.war/episodes/05/). This website is devoted to the Korean War episode of CNN's television series on the Cold War. The site includes multimedia clips, an interactive map of the war's progress, historical documents, and the full script of the television episode.

History of United States Naval Operations: Korea (http://www.history.navy.mil/books/field/index.htm). Describes the role of the U.S. Navy in the Korean War.

Korean War Fiftieth Anniversary Commemoration (http://korea50.army.mil/). This is the official Department of Defense website to commemorate the Korean War. Its history section contains comprehensive information on all aspects of the war, including a time line, maps, a bibliography, fact sheets, and biographies.

Korean War Maps (http://www.army.mil/cmh-pg/books/maps.htm). This army website contains detailed maps of all phases of the Korean conflict.

Remembering the Korean War (http://www.army.mil/cmh-pg/reference/Korea/kw-remem.htm). This site, maintained by the Center of Military History, contains links to official military histories of the war's battles, plus photographs, commemoration brochures, casualty data, and much other interesting information.

The U.S. Air Force's First War: Korea 1950–1953 (www.afa.org/magazine/oct2000/1000korea.asp). This issue of the Journal of the Air Force Association contains a chronology of Air Force action in the Korean War.

U.S. Forces Korea (http://www.korea.army.mil/index1.htm). This site details the current military situation in Korea. Includes numerous links to other Korean War and military websites.

★ Works Consulted ★

Books

Bevin Alexander, *Korea: The First War We Lost.* New York: Hippocrene Books, 1987. The author argues that the United Nations [UN], and the United States, in particular, won the war against the North Koreans, but lost the war against the Communist Chinese.

Roy E. Appleman, *Ridgway Duels for Korea.* College Station: Texas A&M University Press, 1990. Appleman traces the course of the Korean War under the leadership of General Matthew Ridgway, who turned UN morale, and the war, around.

———, *South to the Naktong, North to the Yalu.* Washington, DC: Center of Military History, 1992. The author presents the story of the "limited war" in Korea from the outbreak of hostilities to the intervention of the Chinese Communist Forces.

Clay Blair, *The Forgotten War: America in Korea, 1950–1953.* New York: Times Books, 1987. One of the most complete military and political histories of the Korean War, written by a prominent military historian.

Eugene Franklin Clark, *The Secrets of Inchon: The Untold Story of the Most Daring Covert Mission of the Korean War.* New York: G.P. Putnam's Sons, 2002. The story of a secret intelligence-gathering raid into North Korea before the Inchon invasion, as told by the naval officer who led the mission.

J.D. Coleman, *Wonju: The Gettysburg of the Korean War.* Washington, DC: Brassey's, 2000. A look at the Korean War battles at Chipyong and Wonju, the latter of which the author compares to the Civil War battle at Gettysburg.

William F. Dean, *General Dean's Story.* New York: Viking Press, 1954. A personal account of the experiences of the highest-ranking officer to be captured by the enemy during the Korean War.

Robert J. Dvorchak, *Battle for Korea: A History of the Korean Conflict.* Fiftieth Anniversary Edition. Conshohocken, PA: Combined Publishing, 2000. A comprehensive history of the Korean War profusely illustrated with black-and-white photographs from the Associated Press.

T.R. Fehrenbach, *This Kind of War: The Classic Korean War History.* Washington, DC: Brassey's, 1998. Taken from official records, journals, memoirs, and newspapers, the accounts in this book reflect the experiences of the ordinary soldier in Korea.

Joseph C. Goulden, *Korea: The Untold Story of the Korean War.* New York: Times Books, 1982. The author explores the roles of both military and civilian leaders in the origins and conduct of the Korean War.

Eric Hammel, *Chosin: Heroic Ordeal of the Korean War.* New York: Vanguard Press, 1981. A detailed, step-by-step account of the Chosin Reservoir campaign, focusing on individual soldiers and small unit action.

Marguerite Higgins, *War in Korea: The Report of a Woman Combat Correspondent.* Garden City, NY: Doubleday, 1951. Higgins relates her firsthand experiences as the only female war correspondent to cover combat in the Korean War.

Edwin P. Hoyt, *The Day the Chinese Attacked: Korea, 1950.* New York: McGraw-Hill, 1990. The author explores how the entry of Chinese military forces into the Korean War turned a "police action" into a perilous struggle between capitalist and Communist superpowers.

Donald Knox, *The Korean War: Pusan to Chosin: An Oral History.* San Diego: Harcourt Brace Jovanovich, 1985. This first volume of a two-volume oral history of the Korean War concentrates on the first six months of the war.

Donald Knox and Alfred Coppel, *The Korean War: Uncertain Victory: An Oral History.* San Diego: Harcourt Brace Jovanovich, 1988. The concluding volume of Knox's oral history of the Korean War covers the final two and one-half years of fighting that ultimately led to an uncertain peace.

Douglas MacArthur, *Reminiscences.* New York: McGraw-Hill, 1964. The bold and controversial general recounts his life story and the wars he fought throughout his nearly fifty-year military career.

David McCullough, *Truman.* New York: Touchstone, 1992. A detailed and revealing account of Truman's life by a Pulitzer Prize–winning author.

William Manchester, *American Caesar: Douglas MacArthur 1880–1964.* Boston: Little, Brown, 1978. A critically acclaimed biography of the brilliant yet flawed general.

S.L.A. Marshall, *Pork Chop Hill.* New York: William Morrow, 1956. A gripping, firsthand account by a military historian who inteviewed the troops who actually fought at Pork Chop Hill.

Matthew B. Ridgway, *The Korean War: How We Met the Challenge, How All-Out Asian War Was Averted, Why MacArthur Was Dismissed, Why Today's War Objectives Must Be Limited.* Garden City, NY: Doubleday, 1967. General Ridgway's reminiscences of his role as commander of the Eighth Army during the Korean War.

Patrick C. Roe, *The Dragon Strikes: China and the Korean War: June–December 1950.* Novato, CA: Presidio Press, 2000. The author, a marine intelligence officer at the Chosin Reservoir, describes how the Chinese entry into the Korean War drastically changed the course of the war.

Martin Russ, *Breakout: The Chosin Reservoir Campaign, Korea 1950.* New York: Penguin Books, 1999. The author tells the story of the U.S. Marines at the Chosin Reservoir and their heroic breakout to the sea.

John Toland, *In Mortal Combat.* New York: William Morrow, 1991. A meticulously researched history of the Korean War by a Pulitzer Prize–winning author.

Rudy Tomedi, *No Bugles, No Drums: An Oral History of the Korean War.* New York: John Wiley, 1993. The story of the Korean War in the words of the soldiers, sailors, airmen, and marines who fought it.

Harry S. Truman, *Memoirs by Harry S. Truman. Vol. 2, Years of Trial and Hope.* Garden City, NY: Doubleday, 1956. Truman recounts his years as president at the end of World War II and the beginning of the Cold War.

Curtis A. Utz, *Assault from the Sea: The Amphibious Landing at Inchon.* Washington, DC: Naval Historical Center, Department of the Navy, 1994. A detailed account of the Inchon landing by a historian in the U.S. Navy's Naval Historical Center. Includes numerous black-and-white photographs.

Stanley Weintraub, *MacArthur's War: Korea and the Undoing of an American Hero.* New York: Free Press, 2000. The author recounts Korean War action during the period that Douglas MacArthur was commander in chief of the UN forces.

Periodicals

James I. Marino, "Meat Grinder on Pork Chop Hill," *Military History*, April 2003.

Time, "War in Asia," September 25, 1950.

B. Gordon Wheeler, "Chosin Reservoir: Saga of Epic Heroism," *VFW Magazine*, December 2000.

☆ Index ☆

★ Picture Credits ★

Cover: National Archives
AP Wide World, 13, 24, 50, 94
© Bettmann/CORBIS, 60, 68, 73, 77, 82
© CORBIS, 95
Corel Corporation, 10, 87
© Hulton/Archive by Getty Images, 16, 19, 30, 65, 85, 92, 98, 100, 108
Library of Congress, 40, 72
© Picture Desk/The Kobal Collection, 105
National Archives, 37, 55, 109
S. Sgt. W.W. Frank/Time Life Pictures/Getty Images, 43
Michael Rougier/Time Life Pictures/Getty Images, 21
© Maj. Earnest A. Staples Jr., USA (Ret.), 75
U.S. Army, 48
Steve Zmina, 15, 29, 35, 38, 44, 51, 56, 67, 79, 90, 101

★ About the Author ★

Craig E. Blohm has been writing magazine articles on historical subjects for children for twenty years. He has also written for social studies textbooks and has conducted workshops in writing history for children. A native of Chicago, Craig and his wife, Desiree, live in Tinley Park, Illinois, and have two sons, Eric and Jason.